Maharaja of Kolhapur Rajah Ram Chuttraputtee

Diary of the late Rajah of Kolhapoor

during his visit to Europe in 1870

Maharaja of Kolhapur Rajah Ram Chuttraputtee

Diary of the late Rajah of Kolhapoor
during his visit to Europe in 1870

ISBN/EAN: 9783337017446

Printed in Europe, USA, Canada, Australia, Japan

Cover: Foto ©ninafisch / pixelio.de

More available books at **www.hansebooks.com**

DIARY

OF THE LATE

RAJAH OF KOLHAPOOR,

DURING HIS VISIT TO EUROPE IN 1870

GATEWAY OF THE PALACE, KOLHAPOOR.

LONDON:
SMITH, ELDER & CO., 15, WATERLOO PLACE
1872.

DIARY

OF THE LATE

RAJAH OF KOLHAPOOR,

DURING HIS VISIT TO EUROPE IN 1870

EDITED BY

Capt. EDWARD W. WEST,

OF THE BOMBAY STAFF CORPS, AND ASSISTANT TO THE POLITICAL AGENT,
KOLHAPOOR AND SOUTHERN MARATHA COUNTRY.

LONDON:
SMITH, ELDER & CO., 15, WATERLOO PLACE.
1872.

CONTENTS.

	PAGE
INTRODUCTION	v
DIARY	1
POSTSCRIPT	94
APPENDICES:	
I. THE DURBAR AT POONA IN 1866	99
II. THE DURBAR AT POONA IN 1868	105
III. THE CEREMONY OF LAYING THE FOUNDATION-STONE OF THE HIGH SCHOOL AT KOLHAPOOR	111
IV. THE *Procès-verbal* OF THE CREMATION AT FLORENCE	121
V. RESOLUTIONS PASSED BY A PUBLIC MEETING ASSEMBLED AT KOLHAPOOR TO DO HONOUR TO THE MEMORY OF THE LATE RAJAH	130
VI. RESOLUTIONS PASSED BY A PUBLIC MEETING ASSEMBLED AT BOMBAY FOR THE SAME PURPOSE	130
VII. A BRIEF ACCOUNT OF THE CEREMONIES ATTENDING THE ADOPTION OF A SUCCESSOR TO THE KOLHAPOOR GÄDEE	132
SUPPLEMENT	135

INTRODUCTION.

A GOOD deal of interest was excited in London and elsewhere last year by the appearance of a Hindoo Rajah, who went to all places of public resort, and seemed to take a most intelligent interest in all he saw. Those who inquired about him were informed that he was the Rajah of Kolhapoor,* a territory in the Bombay Presidency, and that he was of high lineage, being descended from the Great Sivajee, the founder of the Mahratta Empire. Towards the end of the year the papers announced the death of the Rajah in Florence, when he was returning to his native country, and the attention of the public was drawn to the strange sight of the cremation of the corpse of an Indian Prince, according to the rites of the Hindoo religion, on the banks of the Arno.

---

* This name is spelt variously—Kolapore, Kolapoor, Kolhapoor, and Kolhapúr. The spelling in the text is the most commonly used, though not the most correct.

INTRODUCTION.

Under these circumstances, and as the Rajah in question was a man of some mark and more promise, besides being the first Hindoo reigning Prince that ever visited England, it has been thought that a Diary which he kept in Europe—though, perhaps, in itself somewhat meagre—would possess sufficient interest for the general public to warrant its publication. Those who made the personal acquaintance of the late Rajah will doubtless hail the appearance of this little book as reviving memories of one who won golden opinions wherever he went; and those who had not the opportunity of meeting the deceased Prince will be glad to learn the impression made on the mind of such an unusual visitor by what he saw in Europe.

The Diary now presented to the public was written by the Rajah in English, which language he could speak fluently and write fairly. The Editor has merely corrected some clerical errors, and pruned away some excrescences and repetitions of no importance or interest in themselves. As few English readers possess much knowledge of Indian matters, it is believed that a brief sketch of the history of the Kolhapoor State, with some account of its present condition, and of the circumstances which induced the Rajah

INTRODUCTION.

to go to England, will add to the interest and value of the work. The following summary of events will be found as brief as is compatible with clearness :—

The middle and end of the seventeenth century were marked in Western India, as in England, by events of vast and lasting importance. During this period a new Empire was founded, and a people who had lost all sense of nationality were welded into a powerful nation by the genius of one man —Sivajee. The Mahrattas were a numerous and sturdy race, but for three centuries they had bowed beneath the Mahomedan yoke, and their country was ruled by Mussulman kings. In the fourteenth century the lieutenants of the King of Delhi conquered the Deccan, and established themselves as independent rulers in the territory thus acquired. After their first resistance had been overcome the Mahrattas disappear for a time from sight, and their name is hardly ever mentioned by the Mahomedan historians. The whole of Maharashtra was absorbed into the dominions of the three Kings of the Deccan—the rulers of Ahmednuggur, Beejapoor, and Golconda—and the Mahrattas are only noticed from time to time as serving in the armies of their conquerors. Sivajee's

INTRODUCTION.

maternal grandfather and father held high office in the two first-named states, but he himself was destined for a widely different career. Brought up at Poona, under the care of a Brahmin follower of his father's, his early years were passed among people of his own race and religion, and he thus imbibed a spirit of nationality which soon proved contagious. By sporting and plundering expeditions among the Mawuls or valleys running from the Ghauts, he became well known to the inhabitants of those parts, who followed him with implicit devotion, and believed him to be under the special patronage of the Goddess Bhowanee. He then commenced a series of attacks on the extremities of the Beejapoor kingdom so insidious that they were at first but little noticed; but soon his power grew to too great a height to be overlooked, and the resources of the state were put forth against him. One army he all but destroyed, after having killed its general by what Europeans regard as an act of the basest treachery, but Natives consider a perfectly legitimate stratagem. By another army he was hard pressed and all but captured, but he escaped all dangers, and partly by force and partly by guile succeeded in carving out a kingdom for himself. His successes paved the way for the overthrow of the

INTRODUCTION.

Mahomedan kingdoms of the Deccan by Aurungzebe; and such was the spirit he inspired that, forty years after his death, the nation he had created extorted at Delhi, from the great Mogul himself, grants of revenue and privilege which, to use Sir Henry Lawrence's words, " not only confirmed them in their own possessions, but authorized their inquisitorial interference in every province of the Deccan;" and where the Mahratta had the right of interference he soon gained the sovereignty. The nation soon became the most powerful one in India; and, had it not been for the check they received from the Affghan invaders on the north-west, and afterwards from the English, the Mahrattas would have been the lords paramount in India to a greater extent than ever the Moguls were. The numerous Mahratta states still existing show, like rocks left on land by some great inundation, how far their power extended.

At his death, in 1680, Sivajee left two sons—Sumbajee and Rajaram. It would take too long to relate here how the former was put to death, and his son imprisoned by Aurungzebe, and how the wily Mussulmans availed themselves of the dissensions between the descendants of the two brothers. These dissensions grew to such a height as

INTRODUCTION.

to lead to actual conflict between the parties in 1729, in which Rajaram's son, whose head-quarters were at Kolhapoor, being defeated, was obliged to accept the terms offered to him—which were, that he and his descendants should content themselves with the sovereignty of the tract of country between the rivers Warna and Kistna on the north, and Toongbuddra on the south, with some specified exceptions. Kolhapoor and Sattara thus became the seats of two kindred, but separate dynasties. The former is still an independent territory, governed by the descendants of its old Princes; but the latter lapsed to the British Government in 1849, in consequence of the failure of direct heirs to the last Rajah.

The State of Kolhapoor thus constituted did not play a prominent part on the stage of Indian history. In the year 1760 the direct line of Sivajee became extinct, but an heir from a collateral branch of the family was adopted, who, according to Hindoo ideas, carried on the succession as perfectly as if he had been born of the direct lineage. Isolated as they were from the rest of the Mahratta Empire, and from the stirring events going on in the North, the Kolhapoor Rajahs devoted their energies principally to fighting

INTRODUCTION.

with the chiefs in their neighbourhood and to piracy. In the latter pursuit they were so successful that the English, in 1765, were obliged to fit out an expedition * against them, and take away their ports, which, however, were restored in the following year. This step proved effectual for a time; but piracy again grew so rife that another expedition was fitted out against Kolhapoor in 1792, when a treaty was concluded; but the evil was not finally put an end to till the year 1812, when the Rajah ceded his chief port to the English, and renounced piracy, the British Government in return guaranteeing his possessions against the aggressions of all foreign powers and states.

The Rajah, who was on the throne when this treaty was concluded, died in 1812, and was succeeded by his son.

During our war with the Peshwah in 1817-8 the Kolhapoor Rajah showed himself a staunch friend to us, and was rewarded by the grant of two districts, which had formerly been in his possession, but had been wrested from him, and received a further guarantee of his possessions.

This Rajah was unfortunately murdered in 1821. He,

---

* The first Treaty between the British Government and the Kolhapoor State was made in this year.

INTRODUCTION.

again, was succeeded by his brother, a Prince of a fierce and turbulent disposition, who disturbed the tranquillity of the country to such an extent that on three several occasions British troops had to be marched against his capital. Notwithstanding the stringent measures adopted against him—territorial cession having on one occasion been exacted, in addition to pecuniary compensation to the sufferers from his violence and lawlessness—Bowa Sahib,* as the Rajah in question was generally called, remained unaltered, and fresh projects of violence were only cut short by his death in 1837. As his son was quite a child, a Council of Regency was appointed, consisting of two ladies of the family and some of the State officials. This Council, however, soon came to nothing, as the ladies quarrelled,

---

* The stories told of this Prince would be incredible were they not so well authenticated. One of his favourite attendants was the leader of a desperate gang of highwaymen; and the Rajah not only connived at his nefarious proceedings, but sometimes actually joined in them. On one occasion the gang, at Bowa Sahib's instance, robbed his jewel-house that the Prince might secretly get possession of and pawn his own State jewels, and thus gain fresh funds for his debauchery and extravagance without the stigma attaching to publicly mortgaging the jewels. A great deal of State land in Kolhapoor is alienated, and a large proportion of the alienations date from Bowa Sahib's time. On one occasion, for instance, he bestowed some acres of land on a shoemaker, who had pleased him with the fit of a pair of shoes. All that reckless extravagance, wild profusion, mad debauchery, bad faith, bad example, and bad government could do to impoverish the State he did.

INTRODUCTION.

and the more energetic of the two assumed the whole administration. Afterwards a Brahmin official of the British Government was placed at the head of the Regency. Of course in a place like Kolhapoor all these changes and events could not occur without causing much excitement. Men's minds were unsettled, and, consequently, some reforms that were introduced excited suspicion and gave rise to discontent and disaffection. At last, in 1844, the latent sparks burst into a flame. The garrisons of some of the hill forts belonging to the State revolted, and a serious insurrection arose, which had to be quelled by British troops.

These events led to important changes in Kolhapoor. Hitherto it had been looked after by the Collector of Belgaum, but now it was found that due supervision could not be exercised by an officer who resided at some distance and had his hands full of other work, and a British officer therefore was appointed Political Superintendent, and since then a Government official has always been at Kolhapoor, who administers the State during the minority of its Princes, and at other times discharges more purely diplomatic functions. The consequence of this has been that what was the most turbulent district in the southern Mahratta country is now

INTRODUCTION.

one of the most quiet. Order has been introduced where anarchy prevailed. Regular courts of justice have been established, roads have been opened out, education has been spread, and the revenue has considerably increased, while the position of the cultivators and population generally has been much ameliorated. Before 1844 there was but little safety for life and property in Kolhapoor, the State was in debt and almost bankrupt, the revenue was estimated at about 60,000*l.* per annum,. and education was entirely neglected. There is now a large surplus invested in Government securities, the revenue amounts, in round numbers, to 290,000*l.*, or 120,000*l.* if the estates of the feudatory chiefs and other alienations are deducted, and there are no less than sixty schools, attended by 3,724 scholars, of whom sixty-one are members of a girls' school.

In the troubled times of 1857-8 Kolhapoor remained wonderfully quiet considering the elements of which part of its population is composed, and also the fact that one of the H. E. I. Company's regiments at the station mutinied and killed three of its European officers. A brother of the Rajah's indulged in intrigues against the British Government, and was consequently sent as a State prisoner to Kurrachee

INTRODUCTION.

(where he died two or three years ago), but the Rajah himself remained staunch, and the Government afterwards marked their sense of his conduct by conferring on him the Order of the Star of India.

In 1866 this Prince died. As he had no surviving issue he adopted on his death-bed the son of a deceased sister, a lad of sixteen years of age, whom he had brought up as his own son. The young Prince's name was Nagojee Row, but, as usual, he received a new name on being adopted, and was thenceforward called Rajaram. His adoption and succession to the throne of Kolhapoor were formally recognized and sanctioned by the British Government, which assumed charge of the administration of Kolhapoor during the minority.

The political charge of the State at this time devolved on Colonel G. S. A. Anderson, an officer of great experience and ability, to whom much of the improvement above noticed is attributable. He proposed to Government that a special assistant should be appointed to take part in the administration of the State during the minority of the young Rajah, and to superintend the education and training, or, in short, act as the governor of the latter, under his direction. This

INTRODUCTION.

plan was approved by Government, and the writer of these lines, then Assistant Political Agent in the Mahee Kanta, had the honour of being appointed Colonel Anderson's assistant for the purposes in question. A Parsee graduate of the Bombay University was at the same time selected by the Director of Public Instruction to carry on the actual work of tuition under Captain West's superintendence, and a scheme of education was carefully drawn up.

The first step taken was to remove the Rajah as far as possible from the pernicious moral atmosphere ever to be found in a native Palace. His Highness took up his residence at a bungalow near the Residency, attended by a carefully selected suite of servants, and there prosecuted his studies, paying constant visits when his study hours were over to the ladies at the Palace, but invariably sleeping at the bungalow. The change was somewhat irksome to him at first, but he soon became accustomed to his new residence and perfectly reconciled to the change, especially when, on the death of his aunt Aka Sahib, her son and daughter, aged about ten and eight years respectively, and whom the Rajah regarded with more than fraternal affection, took up their abode with him. He married two wives, according to the

INTRODUCTION.

custom of his family,* but this caused no change in the arrangements, as the senior wife, the daughter of the chief of Phultun, was little more than an infant, and the second wife, on growing up, lived with him at the bungalow.

The Rajah, when his education was regularly taken in hand by the Government, was already fairly educated according to native ideas, and had some knowledge of English, so that the task of his instructors was far easier than it would otherwise have been. They were further aided by his Highness's own earnest desire for the acquisition of knowledge, and the pains he took with all his studies. His age was too advanced to admit of a very comprehensive scheme of education being framed for him, and little more could be done than to build on the foundations already laid; but great care was taken to ensure his thorough comprehension of all that was taught him, and, without taking up too many subjects, to give him as varied a culture as possible. He evinced a decided taste for reading, and selections of books were procured for him from time to time, he being encouraged also to read newspapers, and make himself

---

* His grandfather had nine, and another predecessor on the throne eighteen wives.

INTRODUCTION.

acquainted with what was going on in the world. Amusement, too, was not neglected. A billiard-table was provided for him, and after getting a few lessons in croquet he became devoted to that game, and constantly played it with his cousins and attendants. He also fancied cricket on a small scale, but his favourite amusement was shooting. He had an hereditary taste for field sports, which was encouraged, and he constantly went out on shooting expeditions with some of the officers of the Agency or his own people. He was fond of riding, too, and took a good deal of exercise in this way. Having a tendency to corpulence he himself felt the advisability of taking exercise, which generally is most distasteful to and neglected by native Princes.

His personal character was a most amiable one. In disposition he was very affectionate and fond of those about him, but, like many persons of this disposition, he did not possess much force of character, and was easily influenced by others—a trait which caused much anxiety to those who had charge of him. Of course great pains were taken in the selection of his establishment, and as far as possible of his associates, to neutralize this defect; but even those who know nothing personally of native courts may

INTRODUCTION.

easily imagine how far from possible it is to make sure that an Indian Prince's companions and attendants are always desirable ones. The Rajah, however, was very amenable to good advice, and always was most anxious to earn the good opinion of the British Government, and those who feared for the possible results of his weakness of character hoped much from the effects of this counter influence.

The Rajah had a decided taste for the society of Europeans. He used always to come to the band stand when the band played and join freely in conversation with the ladies and gentlemen of the station. He liked also, when the Political Agent or any of the officers of the Agency gave a dinner-party, to come in the evening and listen to music or join in any amusement going on. He even had himself taught quadrilles, which he used to go through with great attention and exactness. This constant association with Europeans gave him considerable fluency in English, and grafted the manners of the English gentleman on those of the native Prince.

At first the Rajah's attention was chiefly directed to purely scholastic studies, in which he made very satisfactory

INTRODUCTION.

progress; but as he grew older it was deemed advisable to initiate him gradually into the conduct of public business, and thus train him more directly for the position he would have to occupy. He was accordingly invited to attend the courts of the Political Agent and his assistants when any case of special interest was being tried, and he regularly on fixed days came to the office of the officer whose especial charge he was under to get an insight into revenue, civil, and criminal work. From being an observer he gradually became an actor, and decided cases himself; and in the beginning of 1870 he was formally placed in charge of one of the departments of the State, known as the Khasgee or Private Department; the work connected with which is of a much more important and multifarious description than would be supposed from the designation. The following extract of a week's entries, taken at random from a diary of the Rajah's, will give some idea of what his mode of life was.

1870.—31*st Jan.*—Left the bungalow at 7.30 A.M. and went with my cousins, tutor, uncle, brother-in-law, and some mankaries * to bathe at Singanapoor for Vishalee. The

---
* Courtiers.

INTRODUCTION.

Nyayadish (Chief Judge) and the Chiefs of Boura and Inchulkurrunjee called at 11 A.M.

After taking our meals twice we left the Palace at about 3.30 P.M. Drove first to Mira Bagh, where we ate some fruit and enjoyed ourselves, and thence returned to the Palace. Returned to the bungalow at 7 P.M.*

1st Feb., Tuesday.—At 3 P.M. drove to Captain West's to see the criminal and civil work, and thence went to the town to see the ladies. Returned at 7 P.M.

Left the bungalow at 6 A.M. and rode to Pryag to bathe. My cousins and brother-in-law came with me. Returned at 9 A.M.

My priest at about 6 P.M.

2nd, Wednesday.—Left the bungalow at about a quarter to 5 P.M. and drove to the racecourse to see the review of the 17th Regiment. My cousins, uncle, and brother accompanied me. At the racecourse General Adams and Captain Frazer were introduced to me by Captain West. Returned at about 6.30 P.M.

3rd, Thursday.—General Adams and Captain Frazer, with Colonel Anderson, called on me at about 5 P.M. Then

---

* This was a holiday on account of a religious festival.

INTRODUCTION.

drove to the town to see the ladies. Returned at about 6.30 P.M.

4th, Friday.—Left the bungalow at 3 P.M. and drove to Captain West's to see the civil and public work, and then took a ride through the camp and *viâ* Aditwar Bridge.

5th.—At 4 P.M. went to the town to hear Daji Bora's Katha.* Returned at about 8 P.M.

6th, Sunday.—At 3 P.M. went to the town, and thence, at 5 P.M., with my mother and grandmother and Ebba Sahib, went to the Kale's house for the celebration of Munj.† Returned at about 7 P.M.

After his accession to the throne of Kolhapoor, the Rajah, as was natural, spent most of his time in his native place, and was but little heard of in consequence; but on two or three occasions he came prominently before the public. Towards the close of 1866, shortly after his father's death, Sir Bartle Frere formally seated him on his gadee at a Durbar held in Poona, and the Rajah even then was able to reply in English to the speech addressed to him on that occasion.‡ In 1868 the

---

* A kind of sermon.

† The investiture of a child with the sacred thread. Members of the Royal Family at Kolhapoor attend such celebrations in families to which they wish to do honour.

‡ The speeches delivered on these occasions will be found in the Appendix.

INTRODUCTION.

Rajah attended at the same place the first Durbar held by the present Governor of Bombay, H. E. Sir Seymour Fitzgerald, and presented to his Excellency an address from the Rajahs, Chiefs, and Sirdars of the Western Presidency, congratulating him on the success of the Abyssinian expedition.* In 1869 the public of Western India were interested with an account that appeared in the papers of his laying the foundation-stone of the High School at Kolhapoor,* now called after his name; and when the Duke of Edinburgh came to Bombay in 1870 none of the native Princes who flocked to meet and do honour to the Queen's son attracted more attention than, or created such a favourable impression generally as, the subject of this brief notice.

It was after the Rajah's arrival in Bombay on this occasion that his visit to England was finally determined on. He had long before expressed a wish to see that country, and at first there were those that fancied this to be a mere sentiment which he did not wish really to act upon, for the obstacles a Hindoo has to overcome, and the prejudices he has to encounter, before going on such a journey are very great. He resolutely however faced all difficulties,

---

* The speeches delivered on these occasions will be found in the Appendix.

INTRODUCTION.

and when the step was sanctioned by the Bombay Government sailed from Bombay, accompanied by the writer of these lines, his Parsee tutor, and a suite of eleven native attendants.

The Diary, which may now be left to tell its own story, commences with the Rajah's arrival in Paris. The events of the voyage to Marseilles were duly chronicled, but, as may be imagined, are not worth transcribing.

DIARY

OF THE

RAJAH OF KOLHAPOOR.

SUNDAY, June 12*th*, 1870.—Arrived at the railway-station at Paris, at about 8 A.M. Went to the Hôtel de Lille et d'Albion. At 2 P.M. took a drive through the city, and saw the following places:—The Place Vendôme, with its Column; the Louvre, with the collection of statues and paintings, which are very beautiful and very valuable; the Palais Royal, the Arc de Triomphe, the Boulevards, the Tuileries, the Parc Monceaux, which is very large and pretty, the Champs Elysées, the Hôtel de Ville, which is a very large and handsome building, and is the Town Hall; the Place de la Concorde, where are eight statues of the principal cities of France; the Place de la Bastille, and the Porte

DIARY OF THE RAJAH OF KOLHAPOOR.

de St. Martin and Porte de St. Denis, which show the boundary of the City of Paris.

13th.—At 11 A.M. went first to the photographer Disdéri's to get my likeness taken. I was photographed in several positions, and then went to see the following places:—The Luxembourg Palace, with its throne-room and gardens, which I liked very much; the Sainte Chapelle, which is a large old church; Notre Dame, which is a large and beautiful church, with doors made of several pretty colours, which I liked very much; and the Hôtel des Invalides, in which is the tomb of Napoleon I. The tomb itself is very large, and is made of red stone. Returned at 2.30 P.M. In the evening took a drive to the Bois de Boulogne, which I enjoyed much. This is a nice shady and beautiful park. There are two beautiful lakes and some waterfalls in it.

14th.—Left the hotel at 8.30 A.M.; drove to the railway-station. Left for London at 9.15 A.M., and reached Boulogne at 2 P.M. At 2.30 left Boulogne and sailed to Folkestone, where we arrived at 4 P.M. At Folkestone sat again in the railway-train, and arrived at Charing Cross Station in London at 7 P.M. We had the sea very smooth in the British Channel. From Paris to Boulogne we had a very rich country on both sides. At the Charing Cross Station Mr. Kaye, the Political Secretary, was waiting to receive

DIARY OF THE RAJAH OF KOLHAPOOR.

me; Sir Bartle Frere was there also. Arrived at my house near Hyde Park at about 8 P.M. We had a good country also from Folkestone to London.

15th.—Took a drive in Hyde Park and Regent's Park, and through Regent Street in the afternoon. Hyde Park and Regent's Park are large and beautifully green. These are very good parks. Many people ride, drive, and walk in them.

16th.—Went to see Madame Tussaud's Exhibition. The statues which are here are made of wax, and are very life-like. No one thinks at first thought that they are statues and not real persons. I liked these statues very much. They are of English and European kings and queens and celebrated men. Then took a drive through Hyde Park. At 11 P.M. drove to Sir Robert M———, to an evening party. Sir Robert introduced several ladies and gentlemen to me. He is a very good and polite man. It rained much to-night.

17th.—Drove by Trafalgar Square and Whitehall to the India Office, where I first saw Mr. Kaye the Political Secretary, and then called on the Duke of Argyll, and afterwards on Mr. Grant Duff, Sir Bartle Frere, Sir Robert Montgomery, and Sir Henry Anderson. Then took a drive through Hyde Park to Kensington Park.

18th.—At 1 P.M. went to the Tower, where I saw the very large armours of several English and French kings, and the implements of

DIARY OF THE RAJAH OF KOLHAPOOR.

the Sikhs, Punjabees, Chinese, &c. Here is a large collection of guns—about sixty thousand. This is the Tower where people used to be beheaded formerly. Anne Boleyn and some state prisoners were killed here. Jewellery is kept here, comprising the crowns of the Queen and the Prince of Wales, and some other kings' and queens' things which are used at the coronation. Among all these things the Queen's crown is the best. At 5 P.M., took a drive through Hyde Park and went to the Polytechnic, where I attended two lectures. I liked one of them about the sand and Suez Canal. There was music at intervals, and the second lecturer showed some magic lantern slides connected with the Canal. Here are many wonderful machines and instruments to show experiments about different sciences.

19th.—Went at 3 P.M. to the Zoological Gardens, where I saw every kind of bird and animal. Among these the lions, rhinoceroses, hippopotamus, black tiger, white bear, gnu, nyl ghau, and seals attracted much of my attention. Thence I took a drive to Richmond Park, which is very large and pretty and commands a very nice view. After taking a walk for an hour, returned at about 7.30 P.M.

20th.—Went to Wimbledon, and called on Sir B. F—— and family. Sir B——, Lady and the Misses F—— gave me a very

DIARY OF THE RAJAH OF KOLHAPOOR.

warm reception and showed great hospitality to me. Returned at 6 P.M. At 8 P.M., went to the Queen's Theatre, where I liked the play " 'Twixt Axe and Crown " very much.

21st.—In the afternoon, went to St. Paul's Cathedral, which is a very large building. It is full of statues of great and distinguished men. It has a gallery called the Whispering Gallery. I was quite astonished to see that in this gallery one can hear distinctly another speaking at two hundred yards distance. We went to the top of the church, which is very high indeed, and we had a very good view of the whole city. I was quite tired when I reached the top of the church. At 10 P.M. went to Buckingham Palace to attend the Queen's ball. I was introduced there to the Nawab Nazim of Bengal, his sons, Colonel Layard, and some gentlemen. I was introduced to the Prince and Princess of Wales by the Lord Chamberlain. The Prince appeared to be a very courteous and amiable man. He spoke to me very kindly. Returned at midnight.

22nd.—At 8 A.M. drove to the Paddington Station, and left for Oxford at 8.45; arrived there at 10 A.M. First we went to see the Vice-Chancellor of the Oxford University, where I was introduced to several members of the University. Thence we went to the theatre, where the ceremony of the Commemoration was to be performed. On my entering the graduates and undergraduates of the University,

DIARY OF THE RAJAH OF KOLHAPOOR.

who were assembled in the gallery, made a great noise—I don't know whether it was in my favour. There were many spectators to see the ceremony. The graduates of the University were cheering whom they liked and hissing whom they disliked. They were making a great noise when the ceremony was being performed. After the Chancellor had taken his seat, he proposed in Latin some great men to be made Doctors of Civil Law. Then all the men who were to be made Doctors of Civil Law, came one by one, and the Chancellor conferred the degree on them, speaking some few sweet words about their actions. Afterwards three students repeated essays in Greek, Latin, and English respectively. This was a very grand sight. I went then to my lodging. At 2.30 P.M., went to Dr. A——'s, where I was introduced to his brother and his wife and some ladies and gentlemen. Then we all drove to St. John's Garden to see the Freemason's Fête. The Guards' band was playing there and many ladies and gentlemen were walking about. Dr. A——, introduced me to Lord Rosse and some other gentlemen. On our way to the gardens we saw Lord Salisbury, to whom Dr. A—— introduced me. Thence went to see several colleges which were very large and old buildings. Very good arrangements are made in them for the comfort of the students. Among them, Christ's College is noted. Many great men were educated there. Near the colleges there are

DIARY OF THE RAJAH OF KOLHAPOOR.

beautiful green compounds* and they put a great beauty to the buildings. Then we went to the Oxford Museum, in which there is a large collection of books for the professors and students. I saw a great many men there to whom I was introduced by Dr. A——. Mr. Phillips gave a lecture in the lecture-room. It was very good indeed, and the reply which the Chancellor gave to it was very good also. Afterwards I went to my lodgings, and thence, at 8.30 P.M., drove to the station. Arrived at the Paddington Station at 10.30 P.M. Dr. A—— and his family were very kind to me in making arrangements for me.

23rd.—At 4 P.M. went to the India Office, and had some talk with Mr. Kaye, and then went to Mr. Grant Duff's room. Drove with him to the Houses of Parliament. After going through the different halls, went to the House of Commons, and sitting in the gallery, heard the debate which was going on, on the Educational Bill. We saw the hall in which Charles I. and Warren Hastings were tried. It is a very large and high hall. Returned at about 7.30 P.M. The House of Commons is a large and good building. The debate was not a very interesting one. I saw two leading men in the House, and in fact, in the whole of England and Great

---

* The Rajah here uses the common Anglo-Indian word for the ground round a house.—ED.

DIARY OF THE RAJAH OF KOLHAPOOR.

Britain—Mr. Gladstone and Mr. Disraeli. At 10 P.M. went to Mr. Pender's to see the telegraphic communication between England and India and America, which was lately completed. The Prince of Wales, the Duke of Cambridge, and many ladies and gentlemen were present. I was introduced to Lady Mayo, Lady Northcote, and some ladies and gentlemen. I was struck at seeing that the Prince of Wales received the answer to his telegram from the Viceroy of India in five minutes. The whole of Mr. Pender's house was very nicely decorated and set up, especially the drawing-room and court-yard.

24*th*.—Went to the Paddington Station at 3 P.M. The train in which we sat arrived at Windsor at 4.20 P.M. From the station we drove in the Queen's carriage to Windsor Castle. After going through several fine rooms we went to the lawn where Tippoo Sahib's and other very good tents were pitched, and two or three bands were playing. It was raining till 5 P.M., but afterwards it was clear and the sun was shining beautifully. I was presented to the Queen by the Lord Chamberlain on the lawn. She made a graceful bow to me and asked me kindly whether this was my first visit to England. She appeared to be in good health, and to be a kind-hearted lady. There were many ladies and gentlemen. When the sun was shining upon the lawn and the ladies were walking there with their different pretty-coloured dresses, it was giving a great pleasure to the spectators' eyes. Swords, daggers, and other implements that belonged to Tippoo Sahib, and that have been presented by the kings and Indian rajahs to the Queen, are in the castle, and some of them are very beautiful. I drove from the castle in a Queen's carriage to the station, and arrived at Paddington at 8 P.M.

25th.—Drove to the Crystal Palace to see the rose show. Many kinds and varieties of rose were placed in order. There was very little difference between them. The Crystal Palace is a very large and beautiful building, entirely made of glass. There are different courts—Egyptian, Greek, &c.—showing their manners and customs. The beautiful Indian Court, and a fine part of the building was burnt in 1865. There are very fine fountains and shops of glass and many pretty things. There are a great many kinds of carriages, which are brought here for show. They are very nice and beautiful. There are, too, stuffed pictures.* One is of two tigers standing near each other, and the other is a fight of a lion and a tiger. They are so good that they look very life-like. There are pictures* of barbarian tribes, and they look also like real ones. Mr. K—— met us in the Palace and introduced his daughter and another lady to me. They accompanied us through the building. There is a place here for

---

* In the Mahratta language the word which generally signifies paintings is also applied to stuffed figures and figures made of clay or plaster.

DIARY OF THE RAJAH OF KOLHAPOOR.

5,000 singers to sing. At 2 P.M. we drove to Beckenham. After taking lunch at Mr. M——'s we went to the cricket-ground, where we saw many athletic sports and races—among which I liked the sack-race much. The two-mile race was very fatiguing. The day was fortunately very clear. The ladies and gentlemen of Beckenham had subscribed for prizes. After the races were over, at the request of the committee, I gave the prizes to those who had won the races, &c. Before the prizes were given, Mr. M—— spoke for some minutes, and then the Vice-President spoke a little. After the prizes were given I thanked the committee for having asked me to distribute them, and told them that I would like to give a cup to be given next year.*

26*th.*—Drove to the Kew Garden at 3 P.M. It is a very large garden, and there are many glass-houses in which cocoa-nut, palm, and the like trees are kept. In this garden small patches of ground with different coloured flowers are kept in very good order, and in consequence the garden looks pretty. The roads are also in excellent order. There is a small fine pond near a palm-house with some ducks on it. This gives a great beauty to the garden. The trees in these houses are very much taken care of; not a particle of air is allowed to get in. As soon as one goes in he feels very warm.

---

* The cup was given and is kept as a champion cup at Beckenham.—ED.

DIARY OF THE RAJAH OF KOLHAPOOR.

We find every kind of tree in these houses. Here are several museums, in which every kind of fruit and wood is found. I was very much delighted with the scenery near the large palm-house. Many ladies and gentlemen were walking in the grounds when I was there. Returned at about 7 P.M.

27th.—Called on the Nawab Nazim of Bengal. Saw him and his two sons and Colonel Layard. Thence went to call on Lady M——. At 3 P.M. drove to the South Kensington Museum, which is full of different kinds of pictures, jewels, &c., given to the museum, which contains every kind of fine work and several kinds of fans. This is a large and spacious building. In the evening drove to the Italian Opera, which I liked. The scenery in this opera I liked very much. In this there is an actress called Patti. She is a very beautiful small creature and has got a remarkably good voice. The whole play was in singing, which was very nice. The Opera House is a fine, large building.

28th.—Called on several gentlemen. We left our cards, as we found none of the gentlemen in their houses. In the evening drove to the Crystal Palace to see the fireworks, which were exceedingly pretty. When the rockets were breaking stars of different colours came out from them. "God save the Queen," and some large flowers shown in brilliant stars looked very pretty. The fountains when the fireworks were let off near them appeared red, blue, green, &c. There were shining balloons, too. All this, and other contrivances, made the fireworks look very beautiful. I cannot write how much I was pleased with them. I have never seen such fireworks in my life. Returned at midnight. The whole Palace was lighted up, and it looked like a blaze of fire on account of its transparency.

29*th*.—Went first to a coach factory, where we saw a great many kinds of carriages, but bought none. Then drove to the Royal Horticultural Society's Garden to see the rose-show. Here were several kinds of rose, among which Marshal Neil was the best. This is a pretty large and beautiful garden. The artificial cascades and small flower-patches, kept in excellent order, and the greenness gives a great beauty to the garden. In the evening took a drive through Regent's and Hyde Parks.

30*th*.—Drove to the Royal Academy at 1 P.M. This is a large building, full of very beautiful and valuable pictures of great men, country scenes, and pretty persons. We saw some, not all. At 1.30 P.M. went to the rooms of the Society of Arts, to attend the East India Association's meeting, which was presided over by Sir Bartle Frere. Mr. Fitzwilliam read a Paper on Cotton. I heard very little of the lecture. After the lecture there was some dis-

DIARY OF THE RAJAH OF KOLHAPOOR.

cussion about the paper among the members. Mr. Dadabhoy Nowrojee introduced Mr. Fitzwilliam and some of the members to me. I think the East India Association is the best means to communicate the grievances of the people and chiefs of India to the English Government. At 8 P.M. went to the Christy's Minstrels, where the actors sang some merry comic songs, and made such funny jokes with one another that they caused the whole house to roar with laughter. The actors showed the skating in a remarkable way. I liked the whole play much, especially the skating.

1st July.—Went to Hunt and Roskell's, where I bought some watches, earrings, &c. Thence to a coach factory, where we saw a great many kinds of carriages, but bought none. In the afternoon, drove to the India Office. Went with Dr. Forbes Watson to his museum, where we saw Indian grains, clothes, minerals, the famous golden chair of Runjeet Sing, ivory and stone pictures,* several kinds of Indian ornaments, tools, weapons, and many other things relating to India. I found every Indian thing here. I was quite surprised to see such a large collection of Indian things. Dr. Forbes Watson told me that many things are not placed in the museum, there not being sufficient room.

---

* See note on page 9.

DIARY OF THE RAJAH OF KOLHAPOOR.

2nd.—Drove to Woolwich to see the review. Arrived there at 3.30. We saw the review from the flag. There were horse and foot artillery and volunteer foot regiments. About forty guns were on the ground. The uniform of the horse artillery was very good, but I did not like the black uniform of the volunteers. The ground for the parade was very good. I did not like the march of the volunteers or the way they saluted the general, but I liked the trotting of the artillery according to the music. The artillery had a horse band of its own. I have never seen such a horse band. General Wood came to my carriage and spoke for some minutes. He showed a good deal of attention to me. There was a great crowd of persons to see the review. In the evening went to St. James's Theatre. This theatre is small, but very pretty. I liked the play, *Paul Pry*, very much. One who was Paul Pry acted remarkably well.

3rd.—Went to Victoria Park. Took a drive through the whole Park, which is large and pretty. I liked the order in which the flowers are kept very much. The people who were walking in the park were astonished to see us natives, and used to make a great noise whenever they saw us.

4th.—Drove to see the British Museum. This building is very large. The museum has got a very large library, which is full of

DIARY OF THE RAJAH OF KOLHAPOOR.

books. Every kind of book is here. We don't know the number of books, but it must be enormously large. Five hundred or a thousand readers attend the library daily. In this museum there are several kinds of fossil animals, minerals, and nicely-stuffed animals and birds, also statues, which are very large. There are many manuscripts of great men. I liked this museum very much, and I think this is one of the largest museums on the earth. I went through the Museum and got a general idea of it. If one wishes to see this museum minutely I think it would take months. Thence we went to see the National Gallery, which is full of costly pictures painted by celebrated painters. Some of them are very beautiful. Then we took a drive through Hyde Park and returned home.

5*th*.—Went to a shop to see the Queen's picture, of which I bought an engraving. Then drove to another shop to see the picture of the present Ministry. It is a very good one, and I bought an engraving of it. I also saw a picture of the Prince and Princess of Wales, with their two children, and the picture of the Conservative Ministry. Both these are good, but not so good as that of the present Ministry. Thence took a drive through the park.

6*th*.—Drove to the Paddington Station. Went thence at 1.15, by special train, to have the honour of having an interview with the Queen. Saw Lord Halifax and the Duke of Argyll, and was

DIARY OF THE RAJAH OF KOLHAPOOR.

introduced to Mr. Gladstone at the station. With her Majesty's Ministers arrived at Windsor at about 2 P.M. In the castle, where the Ministers took their lunch, I ate some grapes. The Duke very kindly introduced me to Lord Kimberley, and I introduced myself to Lord Granville, Sir Barnes Peacock, and a judge who was made a member of the Privy Council. After the Privy Council I was presented to the Queen by the Duke of Argyll, and had an interview with her Majesty for five minutes. The Queen spoke very kindly with me, and was good enough to introduce me to the Princess Beatrice, who was standing by her. Before I was presented to the Queen Colonel Ponsonby showed us St. George's Hall and the Waterloo Drawing-Room, which are very beautiful indeed. Colonel Lidden showed us the Gallery in the castle, which is very fine also. The whole castle is very beautiful and fine. Many valuable pictures and statues are kept in it. The drawing-rooms are very finely fitted up and furnished. They are beautifully floored and painted. I liked the whole castle and its park very much. We returned to the Windsor Station in a Queen's carriage, and thence with the Ministers returned to Paddington. I was quite astonished to see the simple and unpretending ways of talking of the Ministers—especially of Mr. Gladstone. They are very gentle in conversation. They have not got the pride of the Indian officers, though they are the leading

DIARY OF THE RAJAH OF KOLHAPOOR.

men of the English Empire. I liked them very much. I was introduced to nearly the whole of the Ministry.

I was to have gone in the afternoon to the Prince of Wales's garden-party, but could not go according to his command, there being no time.

Drove to Buckingham Palace at 10 P.M., to attend the State Concert. Patti, Neilson, and Lucca, the celebrated singers in Europe, sang to-night. I liked Patti's voice very much. It is sweet and lovely. There were a great many guests—about four or five hundred. The whole palace was lit up, and it was therefore giving a great delight to the people's eye. This palace is very large, and it is beautifully furnished. I think it is one of the best royal residences. The Prince and Princess of Wales, with the Prince and Princess Christian, Princess Louise, the King of Hanover, and other members of the Royal Family, were present at the concert, but the Queen was not there.

7th.—Called on Mr. Bruce, the Home Secretary. I found him very gentle, civil, and polite, though he is one of the greatest men at present. Thence went to see the flower-show in Regent's Park. I liked this show very much. The flowers were arranged in many excellent ways and shapes. The Park is large, and very pretty. Many kinds of fruit were placed for exhibition, and many other fine things. Two bands were playing. Thence drove to Doré's Picture Gallery, where two pictures were very fine. Took a drive through the Park, and walked in the broad walk in Kensington Gardens. This is a broad and shady walk.

In the evening drove to the Crystal Palace to see the fireworks, which were very beautiful. Mr. Lesseps was cheered very heartily. He was entertained by the Crystal Palace Committee. The fireworks were in his honour. I liked the fireworks very much. There were a great many people to see them. It was amusing to see the fair heads of so many people. Returned at about midnight.

8*th*.—At 2 P.M. drove to Lord's Ground to see the cricket-match between Harrow and Eton schools. I liked this play very much. There were crowds of people to see the match. The people wore light-blue and dark-blue ribbons, to show that they had an interest in the match. I was quite amused to see the coachmen wearing such ribbons. The English are very fond of such plays and amusements. Thence we went to see H. R. H. the Duke of Cambridge. He appears to be a perfect gentleman. He is very polite, and free in his conversation. He was so civil and gentle that he begged my pardon for having come later than the appointed time. Thence returned home, taking a drive through Hyde Park.

9*th*.—Went to Waterloo Station at 1 P.M., and thence by train to

DIARY OF THE RAJAH OF KOLHAPOOR.

Aldershot to see the review. Reached Farnborough at 2.30 P.M., and thence drove to Aldershot. After taking luncheon at the "Imperial Hotel," drove to the Parade ground. I saw the Duke of Cambridge and the Prince of Wales at the station at Farnborough, and shook hands with them. The Queen, with some members of the Royal Family, and the Duke, arrived at the ground precisely at 5 P.M. The general commanding the force saluted her Majesty on her arrival. The force on the field—including infantry, cavalry, and artillery—was nearly nine thousand. The whole division marched past, and then the cavalry passed trotting. The Prince of Wales, in command of the Hussars, saluted the Queen when his regiment passed, and went trotting. Her Majesty made a graceful bow to every officer on horse or foot when he saluted her as he was passing. The Queen had on a mourning-dress. She had four fine greys to her carriage. Very few cavalry men were in attendance on her. I had never seen such a large military gathering before. The Queen was cheered as she left the ground. As soon as the cavalry passed, trotting, her Majesty went away. We followed her. We had a very good situation to see the review. I liked the march of the troops very much. I had never seen Highland regiments before. I was very much pleased with their dress. Left Farnborough, and arrived at Waterloo Station at 8 P.M. At 10.30 P.M. went to an evening party at Sir Stafford

DIARY OF THE RAJAH OF KOLHAPOOR.

Northcote's, where I was introduced to some people whose names I do not recollect.

10th.—Went to call on the Prince and Princess of Teck. They gave me a very warm reception. Both of them are very courteous and polite. They are in the Kensington Palace. I saw their children also. They are nice well-trained young fellows. Afterwards took a drive through the Regent's and Hyde Parks.

11th.—Two jewellers, who had made the sword which is presented to Lord Napier of Magdala by the Corporation of London, came to show me the sword at 12 o'clock. It cost 500*l*. The whole sword is made of solid gold, and fine workmanship is wrought upon it. At 2.30 P.M. went to Westminster Abbey, where we saw the Dean. He is a learned and polite man. He has written a book called *Historical Memorials of Westminster Abbey*. Thence drove to Allen & Co.'s house to buy books, where we bought some interesting books relating to India. Went back to the Abbey again. This Abbey is eight hundred and four years old. It is one of the ancient buildings in England. It is a large and very high building. Inside it is beautifully carved. It is full of the tombs of English kings and queens, statesmen, and celebrated men of England, and the men who distinguished themselves in India : such as Sir James Outram and Warren Hastings. I saw the late Charles Dickens's tomb, which has made an addition to

DIARY OF THE RAJAH OF KOLHAPOOR.

those in the Abbey. I saw the famous chair of stone of Scone. It is very old. From Edward III. English sovereigns were crowned on this chair. I saw the hall in which the coronation ceremony is performed. The Stone of Scone is kept under the seat of the chair. While returning home met with an accident. Both of my carriage horses slipped and fell on the ground. I think the accident happened on account of the road being slippy, as it rained a short time before. There was no fault either of the driver or the horses. Fortunately no injury was done either to the horses or to the men.

At 8 P.M. went to the Alhambra Palace. It is a large and beautiful building. The sceneries were very pretty, like real ones. The dresses of the actresses were very fine and costly. I liked the gymnastic exercise of the small boy much. I had never seen such a one before. Two men threw the boy to each other from a distance of ten yards, and the boy used to take hold of their hands. This is a very difficult exercise. The people used to feel when the boy was thrown up. I liked the other thing, which was this—a man was speaking with two dolls. On both sides he spoke, but he used to speak in such a way and in so different a tone from his natural one, that no one saw he was speaking, but thought it was the dolls. He had a wonderful gift of speaking in different tones. On the whole, I liked the play very much.

DIARY OF THE RAJAH OF KOLHAPOOR.

12th.—Called on Lady R——, who was not at home. Then to the India Office, where we saw Mr. Kaye, Sir Bartle Frere, and his brother. Then went to the House of Commons, where we heard the debate on the Irish Land Bill. It was very interesting, important, and historical. Then, with the Marquis of Lorne, eldest son of the Duke of Argyll, went to the House of Lords. This building is prettier than that of the House of Commons. There was no interesting debate in the House. We were standing near the throne. The members of the Government sit on the right hand of the Lord Chancellor, who sits in the middle and puts on a wig. The Opposition party sit on the left of the Chancellor. The House was not full when I was there. We went back to the House of Commons, and heard Mr. Gladstone, and Mr. Disraeli and some others. Afterwards the House was closed for some time, and we returned to our house.

13th.—Went to call on Mr. Disraeli, who could not see me, and then drove to the French Gallery. Some of the pictures were very fine. Called on various people, who were all out.

At 10 P.M. went to the Skinners' Ball, where I was introduced to Admiral H——, his wife and daughter, and the Masters and Warden. The hall was very large, and it was nicely lighted up and decorated. The floor was well covered by silk cloth. There

DIARY OF THE RAJAH OF KOLHAPOOR.

was a large company of ladies and gentlemen. The servants were very nicely dressed. Admiral H—— and his family and the Master appeared to me very polite and civil. The supper-room was well lit up and ornamented. Everything was on a grand scale here.

14th.—Went to a dancing-master to have some lessons in quadrilles. Went then to German Reed's entertainment, where several small pieces were played, among which I liked that in which pictures became alive and spoke with each other. An actress called Fanny Holland acted very well. At 4 P.M. drove to the House of Lords to hear the debate on the University Tests Bill. I liked the debate very much, and the speeches of both parties.

15th.—Called on Lord Lawrence, who was one of the Governor-Generals in India, and who is one of the great statesmen. Then called on M. de Lesseps, who was in the country. At 3 P.M. drove to St. James's Hall to see the assault of arms. I liked the several feats and the sword dance. The men of the 1st Life Guards and the Royal Guards showed different sword feats. This hall is very large, and it belongs to the public. At intervals the band of both Regiments were playing.

In the evening went to the Royal Strand Theatre, where I liked pretty well the play of the *Field of the Cloth of Gold.* This theatre is pretty, though it is small.

16*th.*—In the morning had a dancing lesson. In the afternoon drove to the Workmen's International Exhibition. This was opened at 3 P.M. by the Prince of Wales, accompanied by the Prince and Princess of Teck. As soon as the Prince arrived some man delivered an address, to which the Prince read a reply. Afterwards a gentleman gave a short speech, and read a letter of Mr. Gladstone's expressing his regret at being prevented from coming by a Cabinet Council. There was a great crowd of people to see the opening of the Exhibition. The Prince was cheered at his arrival and departure. This building is very large and new. I think it is being built yet. It was decorated with flags. A platform was raised for the Royal Family and great men. Here was a large collection of various fine specimens of workmanship brought from several European and Asiatic countries. We did not see the things, there being a great crowd. In the evening went to St. James's Theatre, where I liked the play called *Paul Pry* very much. Mrs. Wood delivered a pretty long speech, which was good and eloquent. *A Happy Pair* and the school scene from *La Belle Sauvage* were good also.

17*th.*—Took a drive through Regent's and Hyde Parks in the afternoon.

DIARY OF THE RAJAH OF KOLHAPOOR.

18*th*.—Went to the Paddington Station, and left it at 12 o'clock. Arrived at Windsor about 1 P.M. Drove straight to Mr. V——'s, where we saw Sir Bartle's son, who is at Eton School. With Mr. V—— walked to the cricket-ground, where the boys were playing. This is a beautiful green and soft ground. Then saw the church, in which a very large organ is being put up, and where a great number of boys perform the service; also some class-rooms in the College. The College is a large and good building. Here about nine hundred boys are learning. A boy is obliged to take music-lessons besides his studies. The boys in this school have to study only four hours; they may do what they like in the rest of their time. They are quite free after their study hours. They are under no restriction whatever there. Here seventy boys are scholars who are paid. Mr. V—— was very kind to us, showing us everything that could interest us. At 2.30 went to an hotel, where I took my luncheon. Afterwards took a drive through Windsor Park as far as Virginia Water. This is a very large and beautiful Park. A great many kinds of deer are kept here only to see, but not to shoot. Virginia Water is a large artificial lake. We took a long walk also in the Park. Returned to the hotel at 5.30 P.M. While returning we saw the Prince and Princess Christian, but not very distinctly. Arrived at Paddington at 8 P.M. I have enjoyed this day very much.

DIARY OF THE RAJAH OF KOLHAPOOR.

19th.—Called on various people, who were out. Drove to the London Stereoscopic Company, where I bought some photographs of the Royal Family and some great men. In the evening went to the Olympic Theatre. This is a pretty and small building. I liked the scenery in the play very much, especially the wreck of a ship, the departure of a ship, and the fairy scenes.

20th.—Drove to Wimbledon Common to see the shooting for prizes at 12 o'clock. With Lady Elcho saw the prizes in the Exhibition Tent, and also saw the things put up for sale. Some of them were very costly, and they were for challenge. Things for sale were nicely arranged. Lady Elcho introduced me to her husband. Lord Elcho introduced me to the Secretary and some Members of the Association and some other gentlemen, one of whom showed me some caricatures of the camp. We had some fruit, and afterwards, with Lord Elcho, drove through the camp, and then went to see the shooting. I saw the Irish, English, and Scotch, shooting for the International Shield. They were shooting at the distance of 900 yards. It was a good long distance, I think. The arrangements to show who shot the best were excellent. Then we drove to see the quick-firing. One fired forty-eight rounds in two minutes with a gun manufactured lately, and another man fired fifty-three times in the same time. Both of these guns are like breech-loaders,

DIARY OF THE RAJAH OF KOLHAPOOR.

but they can be fired quicker than them. I was quite astonished to see them firing so fast. We saw also some gentlemen shooting at a running deer made of iron. It runs on iron rails. I liked this shooting at a deer very much. Lord Elcho introduced me to the Duke of Wellington, Lord Godrich, Lord Cairns, and Captain Ross, a great shot. While returning saw Lady Mayo. Lord and Lady Elcho were very kind to me, and took a great deal of trouble in showing me everything that could interest me. The more I see the English the more I know their politeness and hospitality shown to strangers. I will never forget the warm reception Lord and Lady Elcho gave me to-day.

It was very hot to-day. A very large camp was formed on Wimbledon Common. About 3,000 people are living here. There is a large bazaar in which everything can be had; and there is a temporary building in which every kind of refreshment can be got.

From Wimbledon drove to Hampton Court. I am sorry we could not see the Palace, which was closed, it being 6 P.M. There is a pretty, beautiful garden near the Palace. It and its roads are kept in very good order. There is a place called the Maze, which is made of several small roads. If one gets into it he finds a great difficulty in coming out. I think no one would be able to come out in a short time without a guide's assistance. There is a

DIARY OF THE RAJAH OF KOLHAPOOR.

vine here which is said to be the largest in England. It supplies 1,300 bunches of grapes. I liked the garden, especially the Maze, very much. Went to some hotel, where I dined, and returned home at 9 P.M. At 10.30 drove to Mrs. Bruce's evening-party, where the Grecian Ambassador, the Lord Chancellor of Ireland, and others, were introduced to me.

21st.—In the forenoon went to have a dancing-lesson. In the afternoon drove to Wimbledon to Lady F——'s garden-party. There was a great company of ladies and gentlemen. Miss F——, Captain West, I, and another lady, played croquet. We won the game. There is a beautiful small patch of garden. The croquet-ground is nice and soft. Lady and the Misses F—— were very kind to me, and they gave me a very warm reception. They introduced some ladies and gentlemen to me.

22nd.—Went to the Bank of England at 12 o'clock. We saw the Secretary of the Bank, and then, with one of his men, walked through the whole of the building, which is enormously large, and built entirely of stone. We saw the printing process of the notes, and liked it very much for its quickness. Saw also the weighing-machine for sovereigns. This is a wonderful machine. If a pound has not got its proper weight it throws it in a different pipe from that of the right one. There is a large collection of notes and blank

DIARY OF THE RAJAH OF KOLHAPOOR.

note-paper in the store to be used in case of necessity. There is also an enormous mass of boxes full of notes which are of no use. These notes are printed from five pounds to ten million. I saw an enormous quantity of gold bars of which sovereigns are made. The Bank sells notes of the value of one crore and a half of rupees every day, and it receives also every day notes of the same amount. I am told that the Bank has got sovereigns worth ten crores of rupees always ready. Notes are destroyed after seven years. I was quite astonished to see the way in which business is carried on, and such a large exchange of the Bank.

In the afternoon went to the Portrait Gallery in Suffolk Street. There are good and valuable paintings in this gallery. I liked some of them. At 5.30 P.M. drove to the General Post Office. I was very much amused to see the people throwing letters and packages into a box. I liked the way of sorting the letters and of sealing* them. They have got such a beautiful way to seal the letters that they can tell after five or six years the name of a man who sealed a letter. The newspapers and packages are sorted in a separate room. They have got a separate department for colonial letters, &c. Indian letters are sorted in that room. India is divided in several

---

* By sealing the Rajah meant impressing the post-marks.—Ed.

divisions. The Post Office sends and receives a very large number of letters every day. The blind letters are those which the postmasters don't know where to send. There are two men who find out as much as they can where it is addressed from reference books, and write the proper address on it. In fact, the business is carried on here in a most excellent and beautiful manner.

In the evening went to the Gaiety Theatre. This is a small but nice building. I did not like the play very much.

23rd.—Drove to Mrs. Jackson's party at Fulham Palace. The garden here is a very pretty and large one, and is kept in very good order. I liked it very much. The Bishop of London, Mrs. Jackson, and their daughters, were very polite and civil. The bishop is very simple. I enjoyed a walk through the garden very much. This Palace is one thousand years old, and it is a historical place. Some part of the Palace is lately built. There is a small chapel, built by the predecessor of the present bishop. It is a pretty, small building.

At 5.30 P.M., drove to Wimbledon Common to see the review of the Volunteers. We had seats on the temporary stand which was erected. I liked the review very little, but I liked the marching past. I liked the uniform of the Highland regiment very much, and also the red uniform of the cavalry and infantry. The Duke of Cambridge

DIARY OF THE RAJAH OF KOLHAPOOR.

reviewed the troops, but he was not present to see the march past. Sir Hope Grant saw the march past. The Princes of Teck and Saxe-Weimar marched past in command of their respective regiments. I think there must have been about fifteen thousand volunteers and seven thousand other troops on the field.

24th.—Went to the Zoological Gardens. I was very much pleased to see so many kinds of birds, fish, reptiles, lions, tigers, bears, rhinoceroses, elephants, giraffes, hippopotamuses, foxes, deer, zebras, sheep, monkeys, and bison. In fact every kind of bird and animal which is found on the earth is there. I think this is one of the largest menageries in the world. Drove through Regent's and Hyde Parks.

25th.—Went to Reilly's the gunmaker to buy some guns. Bought two fowling-pieces and a rifle. In the evening went to the Vaudeville Theatre, which is small. I liked the play but very little. *Two Roses* was pretty good.

26th.—At 4.30. P.M. went to the India Office, where I saw Mr. Kaye and Sir Bartle Frere. I had a long talk with the latter. He introduced the Tahsildar of the Nizam at Aurungabad to me. He knows English very well. He is a descendant of Vicoji, who was a great friend of Chandu Lall, the Nizam's Dewan.

27th.—Went in the afternoon to the Waterloo Station, and left at

DIARY OF THE RAJAH OF KOLHAPOOR.

3.25 for Walton. Arrived there at 4.15. Drove to Ashley Park to a party given by the Sassoons. I was introduced to several ladies and gentlemen, among whom were Mr. and Mrs. G——, cousins of the Premier. This is a large, beautiful, and lovely park. A band was playing in the grounds, and some singers dressed very curiously sang German songs. I saw the boys and girls of the Caledonian School. They were dressed in Highland costume, and they played bagpipes. The ladies and gentlemen took their supper in a tent which was large and nicely decorated. I ate some grapes and took a little champagne. Some ladies and gentlemen danced Scotch reels, which I liked. At 9 P.M. dancing commenced. I danced the Lancers with Miss S——. The Persian Ambassador was introduced to me. He is a good and polite man. The S——s were very kind and attentive to their guests. Left Walton at 10 P.M.

28th.—Went to the India Office in the afternoon and called on various Members of the Council. At 5.30 went to the House of Lords to hear the Duke of Argyll's speech on Indian finance. The Duke commenced his speech at 8 P.M. and ended at 9 P.M. Then the Marquis of Salisbury, Lord Lyveden, and Lord Lawrence spoke about the finances of India. I liked the speeches, but especially the Duke's, very much, and I was very much interested in the debate. Returned home at about 10 P.M.

DIARY OF THE RAJAH OF KOLHAPOOR.

29th.—Went to the India Office, where I left cards for some Members of Council. Then went to Mr. Green's picture-gallery, where I left my name for an engraving of the pictures of the Derby Cabinet, and an engraving of the picture of the Prince and Princess of Wales's Marriage. Went in the evening to Woodin's. This is a small place. I was quite astonished to see him change his dress in such a very short time. He acts and sings pretty well, but I admire his changing his dress very much.

30th.—Drove to the Paddington Station, which we left at 10.15. Reached Oxford at 12 o'clock. Drove first to Christ's College, and then to Mr. N——'s house, to find him out, but to our great disappointment he was not in the house. Then went to Dr. A——'s, where we saw Mrs. A——, and with her walked to the Bodleian Library. Mrs. A—— introduced Dr. Cox to me, and with him we saw the whole library, which is one of the largest in the world. This library is full of books and old manuscripts of several famous men. The gallery is full of the pictures of English sovereigns and statesmen. Then we went to New College, which is a large building. There is a church here which is beautiful. There are pretty grounds near the College which I liked very much. Then on our way to the "Randolph Hotel" we looked in on Dr. A—— and saw him. I must again remark here that I have never found such hospitable men like

DIARY OF THE RAJAH OF KOLHAPOOR.

the A——s. Both Dr. and Mrs. A—— were very kind to me, and took a great deal of trouble to do as much for us as they could. Took lunch at the hotel, and at 3 P.M. drove to Blenheim to see the Duke of Marlborough's palace and park, which were given to the first Duke by the English. We walked through the several rooms, which are nicely furnished, and have beautiful and costly pictures of the first Duke and the family hung in them. The tapestry pictures of the victories of the first Duke are hung there also. These rooms are splendid and beautiful. There is a large saloon which is the Duke's library now. It was used as a ball-room. There are the pictures of Queen Anne and King William. This is a very large palace, and it has got a large compound also. It does not look beautiful from outside, but inside it is very beautiful. I liked this palace very much. Then we took a long walk and drive through the park, which is some miles large I think. We enjoyed our trip to Blenheim very much. Returned to Oxford at 7 P.M., and left for London at 9.30 P.M. Arrived at Paddington Station at 11 P.M. Blenheim is a very historical place in English history.

31*st*.—Drove to Kew Gardens at 4 P.M. Took a long walk through the gardens and enjoyed our walk very much. Returned at about 7 P.M.

DIARY OF THE RAJAH OF KOLHAPOOR.

1*st August.*—Drove to Woolwich at 2 P.M. and saw how the big guns are made and how the bullets are cast. I was very much pleased with the process by which big guns and bullets are made. I saw some enormously large guns. An officer in the Arsenal showed us how the big guns are made, and another officer showed us several kinds of shells and how the bullets are made. I have never seen such a large Arsenal before. Returned at about 7 P.M. I have seen a very curious gun to-day. I don't know its name.

2*nd.*—Drove to the Crystal Palace at 1 P.M. and saw the Automaton chess-player play chess. It is merely a figure made of some stuff. He beat the gentleman who was playing with him. I was very much surprised to see such a figure play chess like a clever player. I can't find out how he played so cleverly. When he made a mate, he nodded three times, and for check, twice. I have never seen such a wonderful thing in my life. Then we saw how the bees with the queen-bee make honey, also a great many kinds of guns, Sniders, &c. There are many things here put for sale. Everything can be found here.

At 3 P.M. went to Beckenham, to Mr. M——'s, where, after taking luncheon, we played croquet. Mr. M—— has got a nice croquet-ground. We enjoyed the evening very much. Mrs. M—— introduced some ladies and gentlemen who were her guests. Mr. and

DIARY OF THE RAJAH OF KOLHAPOOR.

Mrs. M—— gave me very good entertainment. Both of them were very kind to me.

3rd.—At 2.30 went and left cards on Lord Salisbury. Afterwards drove to Mrs. S——'s party. Mrs. S—— introduced some ladies and gentlemen who were her guests to me. Mr. S—— has a beautiful croquet-ground. We played croquet and enjoyed it much. We won the game. After taking a walk through the garden, which is pretty good, went to supper. Afterwards we had some music. Mr. and Mrs. S—— were kind and very polite to me. I enjoyed this evening immensely.

4th.—In the afternoon, called on Lord Kimberley, Mr. Cardwell, the Speaker and Lord Chancellor. No one of them was in the house. Took a little drive through the Park. In the evening went to the Prince of Wales's Theatre. This is a very gay theatre, though it is a small one. We liked all the three acts, but especially *Dearest Mamma* and *M. P.* Miss Marie Wilton and one who acted the Uncle, acted remarkably well. He was laughing in such a way, that he made all the people burst laughing. The Prince and Princess of Wales were present in the theatre. Our coachman having got drunk, I was obliged to return home in a cab.

5th.—Went to the House of Commons in the afternoon to hear Mr. Grant Duff's speech on Indian finance. I liked Mr. Grant

DIARY OF THE RAJAH OF KOLHAPOOR.

Duff's speech, but I liked Mr. Fawcett's and Mr. Denison's speeches very much. Returned home at 7 P.M., but again went to the House to hear the rest of Mr. Grant Duff's speech.

6th.—Went to Euston Square Station at 8.45 A.M. Left for Claydon at 9 A.M. Changed train at Bletchley and Winslow. Arrived at Buckingham Station at 11.30 A.M. and thence drove to an hotel. With Sir H. V. went to the County Magistrates' court, where we heard two criminal cases. Here in England petty criminal cases are decided by four or five magistrates. Sir H. V. introduced two of the magistrates to me. Then with Sir H. V. in his carriage drove to his house. He introduced me to Lady and Miss V——. I saw two Misses F—— and Mr. Grant Duff. We played croquet in the evening. I enjoyed it very much. Sir Harry's house is large and well furnished. He has very nice grounds near the house. Lady V—— introduced Mr. Max Müller and some others to me.

7th.—Dr. A—— came to-day. I with the Miss F——'s, Miss V——, and Captain West, took a walk to Mr. F——'s. He has a nice pretty small patch of garden. Flowers are nicely kept in several beautiful ways. I liked the garden very much. I heard Sunday prayers at night. I liked them.

8th.—Took leave of Lady and Miss V—— at 2 P.M. and arrived at Euston Square at 4 P.M. Took a drive through the Park and

DIARY OF THE RAJAH OF KOLHAPOOR.

returned home. Sir H——, Lady, and Miss V—— are very kind persons. They were exceedingly kind to me. I had nice rooms to sleep and dine in. I was quite khush* and comfortable there. The V——s made very good arrangements for my comfort and happiness. Sir H—— is the type of an Englishman. I enjoyed my trip to Claydon very much.

9*th*.—Went first to the India Office, and then drove to Wimbledon to Sir B. F——s. He was not at home. Saw Lady, Mr., and the Miss F——s. I had a pretty long talk with them. Mr. F—— is a nice young fellow. He is fifteen. Miss C. F—— played the piano and sang some pretty airs. I cannot help remarking here again, that the F——s are good and very hospitable people. Then called on the Persian Ambassador, who was not in the house. Took a drive through the Park and returned home about 6.30 P.M.

10*th*.—Went to Euston Square Station, and left at 10.30 A.M. for Langholm. Changed trains twice. Arrived at Langholm about 8.30 P.M. In the evening it was very hot. Mr. M—— met us at the distance of twenty miles from Langholm. We are living in the hotel called the "Temperance Hotel."

11*th*.—Several gentlemen called and were introduced to me. At

---

* A Hindustani word signifying "happy."

DIARY OF THE RAJAH OF KOLHAPOOR.

12 o'clock saw our shooting dogs and ponies. At 3.30 P.M. called on Lady Dalkeith, who introduced me to the Marquis and Marchioness of Hamilton. All they, especially Lady D——, are very nice persons. Then took a long drive, which we enjoyed very much. Thence we drove to Mr. M——'s sister's place. There is a very nice croquet-ground here, and a beautiful small garden near the house.

12*th*.—Went to shoot grouse on Mr. J——'s moor at 11 A.M. We had after all good sport. Altogether, we shot nine and a half brace of grouse, and two brace of black cock. It was very hot, and we had to climb very steep hills. I was very much surprised to see the dogs beating jungle like men. They are very nicely trained. They find out the scent very wonderfully. When they see or scent a bird they go very slowly, wagging their tails. They find out the dead bird also in a very astonishing way. We drove as far as the bottom of the moor, and then rode. We did the same while returning also. Returned to the hotel at about 6 P.M. I was very much tired from the fatigue of the day. This is the first time I shot grouse.

13*th*.—Drove in the afternoon to Lord Dalkeith's to distribute the prizes to the Eskdale Volunteers. On my arrival on the ground the Volunteers saluted, and I then inspected the corps. I then sat with Lady D—— on my right, and Lord Hamilton and Captain West behind us, and the Volunteers forming lines before us, and a photograph was taken. Then I read a paper to which Major Malcolm replied. After this I distributed the prizes to the volunteers. Then went with Lady D—— to her house, where I had some peaches. Then we saw the people dancing quadrilles and Scotch reels. I like the latter very much. The ground was nice, green, and soft. I enjoyed this afternoon very much.

14th.—Took a long drive in the afternoon, which I enjoyed very much.

15th.—Went to Longwood to Mrs. B——'s at 4 P.M., where I saw some ladies and gentlemen to whom I had been introduced already. We played the game of croquet twice. I won both times. We enjoyed it very much. We had some grapes and champagne at Mrs. B——'s, who is a nice polite lady.

16th.—Drove to Mr. J——'s moor to shoot grouse. After driving some five or six miles, rode. We got ten brace of grouse. It was hot. Returned at about 7 P.M.

17th.—Called on Mr. M—— in the afternoon, and then took a long drive, which we enjoyed very much.

18th.—Went shooting at about 11 P.M. We got ten brace of grouse. Returned at about 7 P.M. It was cold, and mist and dew were falling.

19th.—Went to Longwood to be photographed at 10 A.M. First I

DIARY OF THE RAJAH OF KOLHAPOOR.

was photographed alone in my shooting costume, and then with Captain West and Nana Sahib, the shooting dogs and men, in the same costume. Afterwards I was photographed with all my men who accompanied me to England, in two positions, one sitting and the other standing. Afterwards drove to the woollen factory, where I saw the process of making woollen cloth. I was very much amused at the different stages which the cloth undergoes. Mr. T—— kindly showed me how the cloth is made, &c. Returned home at about 1 P.M. Afterwards drove to Longwood to play croquet, which I enjoyed very much. I liked the songs which were sung by Mr. S—— with his young girl. I was quite surprised to see such a young girl singing so well. I partook of a peach and some champagne. Mr. S—— is a very good and polite gentleman. Mrs. B—— is a very polite and hospitable lady.

20*th*.—Went at 8 A.M. to shoot at Liddesdale. Changed horses half way. Drove eighteen miles and then rode to Mr. J——'s place. Mr. J—— walked with us when we were shooting. We were very unlucky to-day. We got only a rabbit, one brace of blackcock, and one brace of grouse. The ground was very nice for shooting. The weather was rainy and cloudy. The journey was very tiring and fatiguing. Returned about 7 P.M.

21*st*.—The Marquis of Hamilton and his brother-in-law came to

DIARY OF THE RAJAH OF KOLHAPOOR.

see me at 12 o'clock. In the afternoon took a drive, which I enjoyed very much.

22nd.—Lord Dalkeith and Lord Hamilton called on me to-day. It rained to-day and was very cold.

23rd.—Went at 11 A.M. to shoot with Lord Dalkeith and his party on his ground. We got altogether about twenty-five brace of birds. It was nice and cool. The birds were driven to-day, and we shot them from places purposely made for this kind of sport. I liked driving the birds very much. It is less tiring and more amusing. Lord Dalkeith was very kind and attentive to me.

24th.—At 3.30 P.M. went to Mrs. B——'s to say good-by to her. Saw several ladies and gentlemen there. Thence called on Mr. C——, and afterwards took a walk by the river Esk, which we enjoyed very much.

25th.—Went to the Langholm Railway Station in the morning. The Eskdale Volunteers, with their band, marched before me to the station, where they saluted me. With Lord Dalkeith and his party left Langholm Station at 10.15 A.M. Arrived at Thorn Hill Station at about 1 P.M. Thence in a carriage of the Duke of Buccleugh's with Lord and Lady Dalkeith, to the Duke's place, which is called Drumlanrig Castle, where I was received by the Duke, who introduced the Duchess and his daughter to me. With the Duke and

DIARY OF THE RAJAH OF KOLHAPOOR.

Lord Dalkeith took a walk through the garden, which is very beautiful, and is kept in excellent order. I was very much pleased with the different ways in which the flowers of several colours are arranged. I took my luncheon in a fine room which was kindly placed by the Duke at my disposal. With the Duke and Lord Dalkeith took a drive through the Duke's wood, which we enjoyed very much. Fine summer-houses are built in the wood. They command a very good view of the castle and garden. I am told there are seventy rides in the woods. They are altogether forty miles long. Certainly there are very fine rides and drives in the wood, which is preserved very carefully, and they say there is a good deal of game in it. Then we drove to the Duke's kitchen-garden, where grapes, figs, melons, and such kinds of fruits are preserved in glass-houses. This is also a very nice garden. Returned to the Duke's castle, which does not look very beautiful from the outside, but it is very old, and it is nicely furnished and fitted up. The Duke and Duchess and Lord and Lady Dalkeith were very kind and hospitable to me. They gave me a very good reception, and they showed me every kind of attention. Left the Duke's castle at 5 P.M. and drove fifteen miles, and thence travelled by railway. Arrived at Edinburgh at 10.30 P.M., and drove to the " Clarendon Hotel."

26th.—Went at 1 P.M. first to Holyrood Palace, which is very old and historical. There saw Mary Queen of Scots' and her husband Lord Darnley's rooms. There are the pictures of the kings and queens of Scotland. Thence we drove to the castle, which is also very old and historical. There is a very large gun here, also a crown, sceptre, and some other ornaments of the Scotch kings. These are very valuable and beautiful ornaments. This castle commands a very good view of the cities of Edinburgh and Leith. At 3 P.M. drove by the Queen's Drive and enjoyed the drive very much. It has a good view of the bay and the whole sea. Then we took a drive through the city. Returned at about 7 P.M.

27th.—Drove to Dalkeith Palace at 11 A.M. First went to the garden which is pretty. The flowers of different kinds and colours are arranged in a very good way. Then we walked to the palace, which is an old and very historical place. A great many pictures of the Bucclough and Monmouth families, and of celebrated men, and of Venice and Naples, and some few English kings and queens are hung there. These pictures are painted by noted painters and they are very valuable. This palace is nicely furnished and well fitted up. There is a beautiful park near the palace where the young men play cricket matches. Then we drove to Dr. G——'s at Newbattle where I took my luncheon. Afterwards we walked to Newbattle Abbey, the seat of the Marquis of Lothian. It is a very old and historical place.

DIARY OF THE RAJAH OF KOLHAPOOR.

There is a beautiful garden in front of the abbey. There is also a very large old beech tree, said to be three hundred years old. The G——'s are very kind and hospitable.

At 4 P.M. we drove to Rosslyn Church which is also very old and historical. It is very finely and beautifully carved. Here is the Prentice Column, about which there is a legend. There is a good walk near this church.

28th.—It was rainy, cloudy, and chilly to-day.

29th.—Sir Francis Outram, son of the famous Sir James Outram, called on me to-day. At 3 P.M. went to the Museum, where we saw a great many models of light-houses, steamers, machines, and many kinds of minerals, woods, &c. We saw many stuffed animals and birds also. We were very much pleased with the stuffed animals. Then we drove to the Picture Gallery, where we saw a great many beautiful and valuable pictures of landscape and other kinds. Took a drive through the principle part of the city and returned at about 6 P.M. We saw a very large hospital while we were driving.

30th.—Drove to the railway-station and left at 4 P.M. for Glasgow. After our arrival there drove to a cathedral which is a large nice stone building. It is very high also. Then we took a drive through the principal street of the city which is large, fine, and very mercantile.

DIARY OF THE RAJAH OF KOLHAPOOR.

We enjoyed our drive very much. It was very clear and fine to-day. We are staying at the " Queen's Hotel " here.

31*st*.—Went to the railway-station and left at 9.20 for Loch Lomond and Loch Katrine. Changed carriages at Dunblane and arrived at Callander at about 11.30 P.M. Stopped at the hotel for half an hour to see if it would clear. Unfortunately we were obliged to return without going to Loch Lomond, &c., on account of its being rainy and stormy. In the evening went to the Theatre Royal. I liked the play very much. All the players acted well, but Mr. Buckstone and Miss Robertson acted remarkably well. Miss Robertson is a pretty young person. The theatre is a large and pretty good building.

1*st September.* — Left Glasgow at 4.30 P.M. and arrived at Edinburgh at 5.30 P.M. Returned immediately to' the hotel.

2*nd*. — Drove to the railway-station and left for Brechin at 8.40 A.M. Changed carriages at Perth and the Bridge of Dun. At the latter place Mr. A——, Colonel A——'s* brother, met us. From the station of Brechin drove to Mr. A——'s place to see Colonel A——'s family. Mr. A—— introduced his sisters, Mrs. M—— and Lady O——, to me. I took my luncheon there. All Colonel

---

* The Rajah made this expedition for the express purpose of seeing the relations of the Political Agent of Kolapore, to whom he was much attached.—ED.

DIARY OF THE RAJAH OF KOLHAPOOR.

A——'s relatives were very glad to see me, and they gave me a hearty reception. Colonel A——'s mother, who is above eighty, was exceedingly pleased to see me. She is a good kind-hearted lady. Colonel A——'s sisters and brother are very kind and hospitable persons. Left the station of Brechin at 5 P.M. Arrived at Edinburgh at 10.45.

3rd.—Went to the railway-station and left for Callander at 9 A.M. From Callander drove to the "Trossach's Hotel," where I took my luncheon. Thence drove to the pier whence I sailed on Loch Katrine. I enjoyed the scenery round very much while I was driving through the Trossachs. I enjoyed sailing on Loch Katrine also. One sees good sceneries while sailing on the lake. I passed by Loch Vennachar and Achray, the Bridge of Turk, and Duncraggan before I drove through the Trossachs. It was windy but fine when we sailed through Loch Katrine. Our steamer started from the pier at about 2.30 P.M., and arrived at Stronachlachar Pier at about 3.30. Thence we drove to the Pier of Inversnaid, when it rained. Stopped for half an hour. I saw the Inversnaid Fall here. Our steamer started from the Inversnaid Pier at about 4 P.M. and reached Balloch at about 6 P.M. It rained heavily for about an hour, but afterwards cleared off very well. The sceneries around Loch Lomond are exceedingly beautiful and charming. After it

DIARY OF THE RAJAH OF KOLHAPOOR.

cleared up I enjoyed my sailing and the scenery round the loch immensely. Small picturesque islands in the lake give great pleasure to one's eyes. Mr. B—— and Mr. and Miss S—— were tourists with us. Left Balloch at 6.30 and arrived at Edinburgh at about 10 P.M. I enjoyed my trip to the lakes very much. I have never seen such pretty and charming scenery before.

4th.—Took a drive in the neighbourhood of the city which we enjoyed very much.

5th.—Sir A. Grant and Dr. Bühler called on me in the afternoon. I had a long conversation with them. Drove with Sir Alexander to the New Club. It is a nice large building, and the arrangements in it are very good. It is richly furnished. The rooms in it are very large. Then drove to call on Sir Francis Outram, who was out. Left from the Prince's Street Station for Liverpool at 9.30 P.M.

6th.—Arrived at the station of Liverpool at 6 P.M. and immediately drove to the "Washington Hotel." Drove to the Town Hall at 11.30 when Mr. S—— introduced the Mayor of Liverpool and another gentleman. Mr. Mayor with the other gentleman kindly showed us the whole Town Hall and the Exchange. The former is a large stone building. The drawing-room and some other such rooms are nicely furnished, and pictures of the English kings are hung in them. The mayor's office is here. The Exchange is also

DIARY OF THE RAJAH OF KOLHAPOOR.

a fine large stone building. Here the merchants come every day and discuss mercantile subjects. Then Mr. Mayor took us to the dock, which is so large and so nicely and conveniently built that it lets ships of very large size come in. The store-house for import goods is a large stone building. We saw several kinds of things which are imported, such as rice, sugar, &c. One of the storeys of this building commands a very good view of the river. Many kinds of spirits are imported here. · Before this we drove to St. George's Hall, which is a fine large building. In it there are courts of justice. There is a large hall in which Mr. Gladstone's and some other eminent men's statues are. In this hall there is a very large organ. In the building British Association and other such meetings are held. Liverpool is said to be one of the largest ports and mercantile cities of England. Many fine and large public buildings give great beauty to the city. In my opinion it is a very fine city. Leaving Mr. Mayor at the Town Hall, returned at about 2 P.M. Mr. Mayor is a very kind man. He takes delight in showing everything which will interest the stranger.

At 7 P.M. went to the theatre, which is large and pretty good. The actors acted well, especially Leah. The schoolmaster also acted very fine. I was much affected with the latter part of the play.

7th.—Left Liverpool at 11.30 A.M. Arrived in London at 5.30 P.M.

DIARY OF THE RAJAH OF KOLHAPOOR.

8th.—Drove in the afternoon to the Workmen's Exhibition. This is a very large building, with a glass roof. Every kind of thing from every country in the world was shown there. Many of the things were pretty and valuable, and of very good workmanship. I made some purchases here. I was very much pleased with the things and with the arrangements by which they are shown.

Went in the evening to the Princess's Theatre, which is a nice small theatre. The scenery in the play was very pretty, especially the house catching fire was extraordinary and beautiful, and at the same time it was difficult to make such a scene. I liked the last piece, called the *Happy Man*, very well. He who acted for the Happy Man acted remarkably well. He spoke Irish very well also.

9th.—Drove to see the talking machine. It speaks distinctly what is dictated to it. A lady plays it according to the words and sentences which are dictated to it. With the assistance of the lady it speaks well and pronounces also well. It can speak any words in any language. It is a very wonderful thing that such a machine speaks so well. Then we drove to a place where a map of the seat of war on a very large scale is shown. Every important place on the Rhine and in the neighbourhood is shown. One gets a very good idea of the seat of war by looking at it.

10th.—Left the Victoria Station at 12 o'clock for Brighton.

DIARY OF THE RAJAH OF KOLHAPOOR.

Changed carriages at Haywood Heath. Arrived at Brighton at 2.30 P.M. Drove to the "Grand Hotel," which is a fine and very handsome building. Afterwards took a drive by the sea-shore and through the principal part of the city, which is fine-looking, and leaves a good impression on the stranger's mind. In this city there are a good many handsome and fine buildings. Brighton is one of the best watering and healthy places in England. A great many people come here in summer. There were a great many people at this time. Left for London at 5 and arrived at Victoria Station at 6.25 P.M.

11*th*.—Took a drive in Regent's and Hyde Parks.

12*th*.—Drove to Charing Cross at 11 A.M., embarked at the Pier, and sailed with all my attendants along the Thames to Sheerness to see the *Great Eastern*. Reached Sheerness at about 3.30 P.M. We got a very good idea of the extent of London while sailing through the river, and we saw the beautiful scenery also about the banks of the river. We saw the officer in charge of the *Great Eastern* on entering her. A quartermaster showed us everything in the ship which could interest us. The length of the ship is nearly 700 feet, and height about 25 or so. The engine and the screw together have got the power of 2,800 horses. She has got a great number of boats hanging on both sides, and, besides, she has got one or two large steamers about her. The saloons and cabins are nicely furnished and decorated. There are three large tanks in her to keep the telegraph cable in. They contain cable of the length of three thousand and a half* miles. She has got five hundred men as crew, and carries three thousand passengers besides. She is an enormously large vessel. She is said to be the largest in the world. We had chartered a small steamer called the *Nymph*. I disembarked from her at the Sheerness Pier at about 5 P.M. and walked to the railway-station, which we left at 5.18 for London. Arrived at Victoria Station at 7.45 P.M.

13*th*.—Drove to Euston Square, which we left at 5 P.M. for Liverpool. Arrived at about 10.15 and went to the " Washington Hotel."

14*th*.—Took a little drive and then drove to St. George's Hall, where I was received by the Mayor and his wife, to whom the former introduced me. The Mayor also introduced me to Sir Walter Elliot, who knew my grandfather and the Kolhapoor territory very well. Then we all went to luncheon, where I had some champagne and grapes. The Mayor proposed the Queen's health, which was drunk with great enthusiasm. Then we went to the large hall where the Mayor received his guests. In this hall Mr. Mayor came in state after all had taken their seats and made a speech before he unveiled the

---

* *i.e.* 3,500 miles.

DIARY OF THE RAJAH OF KOLHAPOOR.

statue of Mr. Gladstone, in which he praised the Premier and his abilities of administering the country as a statesman, comparing him with other celebrated men whose statues are in the hall. Then Professors Huxley and Rolleston. The former spoke in favour and the latter against the Premier. * This is a very large hall, which is convenient and nicely fitted for such public occasions. There was a great crowd of people in the hall. I think the statue is much like Mr. Gladstone. The Mayor addressed some lord, me, and the whole company both times when he spoke and when he proposed the Queen's health. The Mayor's speech was frequently cheered. In the luncheon room Sir Roderick Murchison was introduced to me, and in the hall Professor and Mr. Huxley.

At 8 P.M. went to the Philharmonic Hall to hear Professor Huxley's speech. First Professor Stokes gave up the chair to Professor Huxley, who made a long scientific speech for full an hour and a half. His speech was liked by all the people very much. Afterwards Lord Derby proposed a vote of thanks to the Professor for his admirable speech, and the Mayor seconded the proposition. I was introduced to Lord Derby, and I saw Sir Stafford Northcote. This is a very good hall also for such speeches. There was a very large audience.

---

* It need hardly be mentioned that this was a mistake of the Rajah's.

DIARY OF THE RAJAH OF KOLHAPOOR.

15th.—Went to St. George's Hall at 11 A.M. to attend the Geographical meeting of the British Association. First Sir Roderick Murchison gave a speech in general as regards the new discoveries and what the Royal Geographical Society did last year. Then Sir Henry Rawlinson read a paper on Paradise which was commented on by his brother and others. Mr. George Campbell then gave a speech on the Geology* and races of India which was commented on by some gentlemen. I like Mr. Campbell's speech, which was given in a distinct, clear tone, very much. Sir Roderick's speech was very good also. I spoke a few words as regards Mr. Campbell's speech, and then Sir Stafford Northcote and Lord Sandon spoke. We returned at 3 P.M.

At 8.30 P.M. drove to the Town Hall for the Mayor's ball. I was received by the Mayor and Mrs. H——. I danced a quadrille and lancers with Mrs. H——, who introduced several ladies and gentlemen to me, such as Colonel Grant, the celebrated traveller through Central Africa, and others. The Mayor issued one thousand tickets for to-day's ball. The whole Town Hall was nicely furnished and handsomely decorated. A great many valuable pictures were hung in the state rooms. I cannot help remarking here that the Mayor and Mrs. H—— were very kind and attentive to their guests, and

---

* This should be Physical Geography.

DIARY OF THE RAJAH OF KOLHAPOOR.

they acted the part of hosts remarkably well. I enjoyed this evening very much.

16th.—Went to St. George's Hall to hear the geographical discussion at 11 A.M., where I heard Mr. Taylor's paper on the Indian ports and harbours, and the discussion on it. Then, at 2.30, drove to the Museum, where there is a large collection of stuffed animals, and birds, and of minerals. There are also different kind of arms, and clay materials. I was very much pleased with the things I saw here. Returned to our hotel at 3 P.M. At 5 P.M. drove in a splendid and gorgeously ornamented carriage of the Mayor's, which he kindly sent for us, to the Mayor's official residence to spend that evening with him and Mrs. H——. I took my dinner in a room which was placed at my disposal, and took some champagne and grapes with the Mayor and his guests. Here the Mayor and Mrs. H—— showed every attention to me. At 9 P.M. drove with the Mayor and Mrs. H—— to the Town Hall for the Mayor's ball. The Town Hall was lit up and furnished as it was yesterday. Mrs. H—— introduced some ladies and gentlemen to me, among whom was Mr. Jeff. Davis, late President of the Southerners. I danced with some ladies. About two thousand people were present at to-night's ball. I enjoyed this evening immensely.

17th.—Mr. Mayor came to our hotel at 11 A.M. Drove with him

DIARY OF THE RAJAH OF KOLHAPOOR.

in his carriage to the Town Hall, where he introduced two magistrates of the city of Liverpool. We saw in a magistrate's court, which was nicely arranged, four or five cases decided in five minutes. I was very much struck to see cases decided in this country in such a short time. Then we went to see the working of the fire steam-engine, which is worked by steam instead of by men. It will put a stop to any violent fire. It takes only twenty minutes to have full force. I was very much interested with the working of the engine, and the way by which policemen save people from perishing by fire. I was very much astonished to see a bottle of some liquid which is thrown to set a house on fire or to produce a fire in the army, &c. It is a very destructive and dangerous thing. The Fenians are said to have used such bottles. Then we saw cellars in which prisoners are kept before they are convicted, and the guns which the police use on necessary occasions. The head of the police showed us what I have written about the steam engine, &c.

We then drove to see the Queen's Equestrian Statue, which is going to be placed before St. George's Hall. It is cast in bronze by Mr. Thorneycroft, a sculptor. In my opinion it is very much like her Majesty. The Queen is shown wearing military uniform, with the badge and order of the Garter. Then, with Mrs. H—— and Miss B——, drove to the Mayor's official residence, where I had some

DIARY OF THE RAJAH OF KOLHAPOOR.

grapes and champagne while the others took their luncheon. Mr. H—— has a very nice little girl. I got a very warm reception from Mrs. H——. Then in the Mayor's carriage drove to the Town Hall. Thence with the Mayor went to the pier, where we embarked in a small tug, and sailed to New Brighton. We got a very good idea of Liverpool and its docks while sailing along the river. We disembarked at New Brighton. There is a very nice promenade there, where one gets a very good and fresh sea-breeze. Embarked again and arrived at Liverpool at 3.30 P.M. Drove to the hotel, where the Mayor took his leave. Left Liverpool at 4.15 P.M., and arrived at Manchester at 5.45 P.M., and drove to the "Queen's Hotel." At 7 P.M. drove to the theatre to see *Richard III.* played. It is a small, but pretty good theatre. The scenery and the dresses were got up very nicely. I liked the play. A man who acted Richard III. acted nicely.

I cannot help remarking here, that the Mayor and Mrs. H—— (at Liverpool) gave me a very good reception, and showed me every attention, and did their best to comfort and please me.

18*th*.—I took a drive through the principal parts of the city and then drove through the country outside. Manchester is a large and fine town. Some of the buildings in it are very fine and large, but I think the factories spoil the beauty of the town.

DIARY OF THE RAJAH OF KOLHAPOOR.

19th.—Drove to see a cotton-mill at 12.30, and saw how the fine yarns are made out of dirty cotton. The head of the factory was introduced to me and showed us everything. At 3 P.M. went to an iron factory where railway-boilers, wheels, and other kinds of machines are made. The whole work is done in a short time with great ease by the aid of steam-engines. In the evening went to the Royal Theatre where we saw Shakspeare's play *As You Like It* acted. I liked the play very much. Miss Robertson, who acted the part of Rosalind, acted remarkably well. A farce called *Box and Cox* was very amusing. Mr. Buckstone acted very well in it.

20th.—At 11 A.M. drove to a silk factory. The head of the factory showed us how the dhotees and plain and embroidered silk cloths are made. I was very much pleased with the way these things are made. Some of the silk cloths were very pretty and handsome. Embroidered cloths are very difficult to be made. All the dhotees were made for India, the plain silk cloths were for lining, and the embroidered ones for tables, &c. The whole work was done by machinery with human assistance. I got some pretty patterns of silk cloths and embroidery. Returned to our hotel and thence to the railway-station, which we left at 1.30 for Inverness.

21st.—Arrived at Inverness at 8.30 and drove immediately to a house in Church Street. Drove in the afternoon to the cathedral, which is a fine and pretty small building. It has been lately built. Then we drove to a hill which commands a very good view of Inverness and its environs. There are many tombs also there. There is a small patch of garden. Then we drove to the islands in the Ness where we took a walk, which we enjoyed very much.

22nd.—Went at about 2 P.M. to see the games. On the road Mr. Mackintosh, member for the County of Inverness and his brother-in-law were introduced to me. We saw the games from a stand which was erected temporarily. Sir David Wedderburn and several other gentlemen were introduced to me there. The games were such as these:—Highland dance and sword dance, throwing hammers, and putting stones, long and short running races. I liked the Highland dress and bagpipes very much. I think that dress is more soldier-like than anything else.

In the evening went to the ball where several ladies and gentlemen were introduced to me, among whom was Sir George Lawrence, brother of Lord Lawrence. I danced the lancers with Mrs. M——. The ball-room was large and well lit up. There were about six hundred people there. Many gentlemen wore the Highland costume, which gave a great beauty to the ball-room. I liked the Scotch reels very much.

23rd.—Drove at 1.30 P.M. to Mr. M——'s, where I was introduced to some ladies and gentlemen, among the latter of whom were some Indians. Took a walk with Mr. M—— in his lawn and small garden. The lawn is very soft and pretty. I took some champagne and grapes while they all took their lunch. Mr. M—— was very kind to us. Then we drove to see the games, which were such as these :— sword and plain dancing with bagpipes, velocipede races, &c. The latter was the most amusing of all the games. One of the four men tumbled down while running the race. There was a great crowd of people to see the games. Some ladies and gentlemen were introduced to me. Among them also some, or nearly all, were Indians. The day was charming. Thence took a drive for an hour and went at 5.30 to see the bazaar, where I made some purchases. The whole hall was nicely and beautifully decorated. There were half-a-dozen stalls in which things were well arranged. I made purchases from all the stalls. The ladies gave me a very warm reception and some of them gave me bouquets of flowers.

At 10.30 went to the ball, where I danced the lancers and quadrilles. There was more people than there were yesterday.

24*th*.—Drove in the afternoon to Culloden Moor where we saw the field on which the battle was fought in 1745, between the English and Scotch, and the stone on which the Duke of Cumberland stood and commanded the English army. On the field there is a mass of

DIARY OF THE RAJAH OF KOLHAPOOR.

stones and on a stone there is an inscription as follows:—
"Culloden 1745." Thence taking a drive, which we enjoyed immensely, returned at 5.30 P.M.

25th.—Drove in the afternoon to a hill and walked to the top of it. A fort was said to be on the top of the hill, but there are no relics of it at present. Some kinds of stones are found there now. They are said to be vitrified ones. A good view of the Moray Firth and the neighbourhood is obtainable from the top of it. The road to the top of the hill is very steep and slippery.

26th.—Drove to the railway-station and left for Nairn at 12.45. At the station met Mr. W—— and his son. Thence with them we drove to Cawdor Castle where Mr. W—— introduced me to Lady E—— and her sister. One of Lady E——'s servants showed us everything in the Castle which was worth seeing. The Castle is very old and it is a historical place. Two or three rooms are hung with tapestry which is very good. There is a dungeon here in which we saw a stem of a tree with which a legend is connected. A good view is obtained from the top of the Castle. There are very curious fire-places. There are good carvings round them. I took my luncheon in a room which was placed at my disposal by Lady E——. We then took leave and went to Mr. W——'s at Nairn. Mr. W—— introduced his children to me. Mrs. W—— is a very kind and

DIARY OF THE RAJAH OF KOLHAPOOR.

hospitable lady. Left at 5.30 and arrived in Inverness at 7 P.M. We saw a church in which Mr. W—— preaches. It is a small, but pretty church.

27th.—Went to Major R——'s at Kilravock at 11 A.M. I took my lunch in a room which was placed at my disposal, and afterwards had some champagne and grapes with Major R—— and his family. Then with him we went out shooting at 2.30 P.M. We shot altogether two brace of hares and four-and-a-half brace of partridges. I myself shot a brace of hares and a brace of partridges. The day was charming. I walked the whole time. I was very much tired after this day's excursion. Major R—— has got a large estate and he has a beautiful avenue round the Castle, which is very old and built in the old fashion.

28th.—Left Inverness Station at 10.18 A.M., and arrived at Fochabers at about 12.30. Thence drove in the Duke of Richmond's carriage to Gordon Castle, at the entrance of which I was received by the Duke who introduced me to the Duchess. Took a walk with the Duke in his garden and the park. The garden is very pretty and large. It is kept in the most excellent order. The flowers and creepers are arranged very well. The park also is very large, and in it there is a very large lime-tree, which is said to be at least one hundred years old. There is a pond, which is pretty large, with swans

DIARY OF THE RAJAH OF KOLHAPOOR.

on it. Took lunch in a room which was placed kindly at my disposal. Took a walk with the Duke in the other garden. It is in the hills. It is also large and pretty. It commands a very good view of the neighbouring country. There are small summer-places in these gardens from which also a good view is obtained. Then saw the farm and the keepers' houses. The castle is a large, old-fashioned building. It dates from very old time. Some portion of it has been built lately. The rooms in it are nicely fitted up. The Duke's office-room is full of different kinds of arms and armour. It is a very large and good collection of arms. The Duke was very kind and attentive to me. Drove to Fochabers in the Duke's carriage and left at 4.9 P.M. At Forres, I met Mr. Mackintosh, who introduced some gentlemen to me. Then we went in the same carriage to Inverness, where we arrived at 6.30 P.M.

29th.—Drove to the Inverness Pier at 6.45 A.M., and embarked on board the steamer *Gondolier*, in which the arrangements were very nice and comfortable. The steamer was beautifully furnished. The scenery at some parts of the canal was charming and beautiful. Our steamer started at 7 A.M., and arrived at Banavie at 2.30 P.M. Thence drove a mile and again embarked on board the steamer *Pioneer*, which was not so pretty as the *Gondolier*. Arrived at Oban at 7.45 P.M., and drove to the "Great Western Hotel" where we stayed the night.

DIARY OF THE RAJAH OF KOLHAPOOR.

Ben Nevis is the highest mountain in Scotland, and it is 4,000 feet high. We sailed to-day through several lakes, such as Lochs Ness, Lochy, and Eil, and passed by Fort Augustus and Fort William. We could not see much scenery on account of its being hazy in the latter part of the day. Oban is a large place. Its bay is very pretty.

30*th*.—Drove to Oban Pier at 7.45 A.M. Our steamer, the *Chevalier* left the pier at 8.30 A.M., and arrived at Crinan at 10.30 A.M. This steamer was good and comfortable also. Sailed through the Crinan Canal in a small tug. The scenery about the canal was very pretty. Arrived at Ardrishaig at 12.30. Then went to a hotel where I took my lunch. Drove to Ardrishaig Pier at 3.30. P.M. Our steamer, the *Iona*, left at 4 P.M., and arrived at Greenock at 8 P.M. Left Greenock by train at 9 P.M., and arrived at Glasgow at 10 P.M. Drove immediately to the "Queen's Hotel." The *Iona* is also a large and handsome steamer. They have got locks in the Caledonian and Crinan Canals to raise or lower the steamer according to the level of the water.

1*st October*.—Drove to the station and left for London at 5.55 P.M.

2*nd*.—Arrived at Euston Square Station at about 5 A.M. In the afternoon took a drive which we enjoyed much.

DIARY OF THE RAJAH OF KOLHAPOOR.

3rd. Drove to a photographer's, where my likeness was taken in different positions. Took a drive on the Thames Embankment. An enormous sum of money has been spent on this embankment. It is a broad way, and there is a good avenue of trees on one side of it.

In the evening went to Drury Lane Theatre, where I saw *Amy Robsart* played. The scenery and dresses were beautiful. I liked them immensely. I cannot write how pretty these dresses and scenery were. The theatre is very large and handsome.

4th.—Drove in the afternoon to the British Institution. There is a large collection here of paintings drawn by members of the Royal Family and painters. The money which is got by selling pictures goes to aid the German sick and wounded in the war. I bought some pictures painted by the royal painters. Then we went to see the Holborn Viaduct works, which are very large, and of good strong workmanship. We saw the Meat Market on our way. It is an enormously large and fine strong stone building. Returned at about 6 P.M. We celebrated our *Dussara** here.

5th.—Drove to the South Kensington Museum, where we saw a great many pictures painted by famous painters, such as Landseer and others. They are very valuable. There are a great many kinds

---

* A Hindoo feast, the advent of which in old days used to be the signal for resuming military operations which had necessarily to be suspended during the rainy season.—ED.

DIARY OF THE RAJAH OF KOLHAPOOR.

of minerals, glasses, miniatures, enamels, and many Indian things. Every kind of beautiful workmanship is here. I cannot give the names of the things which are here. In the evening went to the Queen's Theatre, where the *Midsummer Night's Dream* was played. The dresses and scenery were something wonderful. Mr. Phelps acted remarkably well.

6*th.*—Went to the Stereoscopic Company, in Regent Street, and bought some photographic views of London.

7*th.*—Went to Price's Candle Factory, where we were received by the manager, who showed us how the candles and soap are made. Mr. Child showed us how the night-lights are made. I had never seen the night-lights before. I was very much pleased with the process by which the above things are made. I liked the coloured candles very much. We saw how they are packed also.

In the evening went to the Prince of Wales's Theatre, where we saw *M.P.* and two other pieces played. I liked *M.P.* very much; Miss Marie Wilton acted Cecilia's part very well. The theatre is small, but it is pretty, and nicely decorated.

8*th.*—Went and called on Mr. S—— at 3 P.M., when I saw Mrs. S—— and others. Had some champagne and grapes with them. Mr. and Mrs. S—— are very good, kind, and hospitable persons.

10*th.*—Drove to Croydon House, to see the Archbishop of Canter-

DIARY OF THE RAJAH OF KOLHAPOOR.

bury. The Archbishop introduced me to Mrs. Tait, his children, and some ladies and gentlemen. I took my luncheon in a room which the Archbishop kindly put at my disposal. Afterwards I had some champagne and grapes with the Archbishop and party. With the Archbishop I took a drive through the wood and park about the house, which we enjoyed very much. The preserves and the park are very pretty: I liked the former exceedingly. The house is large, and the arrangements in it are perfect: it is nicely furnished The Archbishop and Mrs. Tait were very kind and attentive to me.

At 5 P.M. drove to Beckenham, and saw Mr. and Mrs. M—— and several ladies and gentlemen. Returned to this house at 6.30 P.M. In the evening went to the Alhambra, where we saw different kinds of ballets. I was quite astonished to see the exercise of the two boys, and to see a boy thrown by one in the air and caught hold of by another; this is the most difficult and wonderful exercise that ever I saw.

11*th*.—I had a tea-party in the afternoon. There were various ladies and gentlemen. They saw the ornaments and toys which I had bought in England and Scotland. At 4 P.M. they took luncheon in the dining-room, where I had some grapes and champagne. The party dispersed at 6 P.M. I had been in the morning to a photographer's, where my likeness was taken in several positions.

DIARY OF THE RAJAH OF KOLHAPOOR.

In the evening took a drive through Regent Street, Bond Street, and Oxford Street, and saw how they were lit up. I enjoyed my drive very much. I liked the way in which the things were put in the shops. Every part of the things were shown to the public.

11th.—Drove in the afternoon to Wimbledon, to Sir B. F——'s. Saw Lady and the Misses F——, and had a long conversation with them. They gave me a very good reception. I have never seen such kind people as the F——s are. In the evening went to St. James's Hall for the concert, which was in aid of the German sick and wounded. Several ladies and gentlemen sang and played on different instruments. I liked the German song, "The Watch on the Rhine." I was very much disappointed at not having heard Madame Otto Goldschmidt.

13th.—Drove to Reilley's, in Oxford Street, and selected some guns.

Went in the afternoon to a shooting-ground, and shot with the guns which we chose yesterday.

In the evening went to the Globe Theatre, and saw *Taming the Shrew* played. I liked the play. Miss Alleyne acted well. The theatre is a small but pretty one.

15th.—Drove to the India Office at 3.30 P.M. No one being there whom I knew, went and called on Mr. W——, and then took a drive in the park.

DIARY OF THE RAJAH OF KOLHAPOOR.

16th.—It was rainy to-day.

17th.—Drove to Euston Square station, and left at 7.15 for Dublin. Arrived at Holyhead at 2 P.M. Set sail immediately, and arrived at Kingstown at 6.45 P.M. The Private Secretary to the Viceroy of Ireland met me at Kingstown. With him went in the train to Dublin, where we arrived at 7 P.M. Then in the Viceroy's carriage drove to the " Gresham Hotel." I was very sick in crossing the channel, on account of its heaving. The steamer in which we crossed the channel was large and very nice.

18th.—Went in the Viceroy's carriage to the Viceregal Lodge at 12.30, and saw the Viceroy, who introduced Lady Spencer to me. I was received by one of the Viceroy's aides-de-camp and private secretary at the entrance. I had a pretty long conversation with Lord Spencer, who is a very kind and courteous man. The Viceregal Lodge is in the Phœnix Park, which is a very large and beautiful park. The lodge is large and well furnished. The Viceroy returned my visit, with his aide-de-camp, at 3.30. The Viceroy's Private Secretary called on me afterwards, and with him we drove first to Trinity College, where we saw the Provost, the head of the College. He showed us the library, museum, examination hall, and a room containing all kinds of models of engineering. The library is very large, and contains 120,000 volumes; the examination hall is very large also. In this hall there is a chandelier which is said to have been used in the Irish Parliament House, and there is an organ, which is large, and was found in one of the wrecked ships belonging to the Spanish Armada. Twelve hundred students are studying in this College. All these students have got their lodging near the College. Then we drove to the Castle, which is a large stone building. It is nicely furnished. The Lord Lieutenant gives entertainments in this Castle during the winter.

In the evening drove to the Theatre Royal. I liked the play called *School* very much. All the actors acted remarkably well. It is a good theatre.

19th.—Lord Monck called on me. In the afternoon took a drive to Kingstown, where we saw a tower erected in commemoration of the visit of George IV. to Dublin. It was rainy and cloudy to-day.

20th.—Drove to Lord Monck's place, called Charleville. We had a very pretty drive. We passed through a pass called "the Scalp," between two hills. There is a legend connected with this pass. There are two hills near Charleville, and as they are in the shape of sugar-loaves, they are called Big and Little Sugar-loaf. Lord Monck introduced Lady Monck, his son and daughters, Lord Powerscourt, and some other ladies and gentlemen to me. Captain West introduced his uncle to me. I took my lunch in a room placed at my disposal

DIARY OF THE RAJAH OF KOLHAPOOR.

by Lord Monck, and then had some grapes and champagne with his party. Charleville is a nice and pretty place. It has got very beautiful grounds and woods about it. Lord and Lady Monck are very kind and hospitable persons. At 3 P.M., with Lords Monck and Powerscourt, drove to Powerscourt House, where Lord Powerscourt introduced Lady P. to me. Powerscourt is a large and very nice house. It is very richly and beautifully furnished. A ball-room in it is very large and pretty. A very good view of the neighbouring country, which is very pretty, is obtained through some of the windows. There are very pretty grounds and preserves in the neighbourhood of the house. Lord Powerscourt is a great shikaree. He had been to India only to shoot. He shot elephants, bisons, and a great many kinds of deer there. He has put elephants' heads and feet, and a great many kinds of deer and bison, which he shot, in a room. I liked the house and grounds very much. Then drove to Powerscourt Waterfall, which is very picturesque indeed. When we were going to the waterfall we saw red and black deer on both sides. The country about the waterfall is very pretty and charming. Lord P—— is a kind and merry man. Then we drove to Bray. We passed through the grounds and preserves of Lord Monck, which are exceedingly pretty and picturesque. The river which flows through them in a valley gives a great beauty to them. Left Bray at 5.30 P.M., and arrived

DIARY OF THE RAJAH OF KOLHAPOOR.

at Dublin at 6.30 P.M. in the railway. I have enjoyed to-day very much.

At a little after 10 P.M. went to the Viceregal Lodge for the ball, where several ladies and gentlemen were introduced to me. I opened the ball by dancing a quadrille with Lady Spencer. I afterwards danced lancers and quadrilles with Lady M——, the Misses M——, and others. Lord and Lady Spencer were exceedingly kind and attentive to me. The ball-room was nicely lit up.

21st.—Drove at 10.30 A.M. to the Zoological Gardens, where I was received by a gentleman who has the charge of the gardens, and where I saw a great many kinds of beasts, birds, fish, &c., such as monkeys, lions, tigers, eagles, parrots. The Lord Lieutenant's Private Secretary met us at the gardens. Thence we walked to inspect the constabulary, where I was saluted by the corps. Walked through the lines. The head of the corps showed us the mess-room, barracks, &c., with which I was pleased. We saw a riding-school and the stable. I was very much pleased with the foot and mounted police, who are strong and well built. I liked the lion cubs in the Zoological Gardens very much, some of them are only a week old. Then we drove to a botanical garden, which is large and very pretty. It is kept in splendid order, and the flowers are arranged in many beautiful shapes. Dr. Moore showed us the hot-houses, which are very nice,

DIARY OF THE RAJAH OF KOLHAPOOR.

and everything worth seeing. I liked the gardens and roads very much. I saw Addison's Walk also. Then, after leaving cards at the Lord Mayor's residence, went to the Museum of the Royal Irish Academy, where Sir W. Wilde showed us a great many antiquities which were found in Ireland.

In the afternoon drove out to Mr. W——'s. Walked with him in his garden, which is small, but pretty. His house is also very nice and well furnished. Had some grapes and champagne there, and returned to Dublin at about 8 P.M.

22nd.—Drove to the railway-station at 6 A.M., and left at a quarter past for Kingstown. Embarked at Kingstown Pier at 6.45, and arrived at Holyhead at 11.30 A.M. We had not a very rough sea. Arrived at Euston Square at 6.30 P.M.

23rd.—It was rainy and cloudy to-day.

24th.—Went to a picture gallery, where there were some beautiful paintings of the coast of Norway. I bought some of the engravings of them. Took a drive in the park. To-day was our Dewallee holiday.

25th.—Drove in the afternoon to Lambeth Palace. This has been the residence of the Archbishops of Canterbury for many years. Some part of the building is very old. There is a tower called the "Lollards' Tower." There is a celebrated prison also, which is very old, and which was used once as a state prison. The palace is nicely furnished, especially the Archbishop's private rooms. There are pictures of the former archbishops in a room. The librarian showed us the library, various manuscripts, and everything worth seeing. The building is very large, and has got a park round it. There is a private church, which is small but pretty.

In the evening drove to the Haymarket Theatre, where we saw *The Rivals*, and a farce called *Uncle's Will*. I liked both of the plays very much; Miss Robertson, Mr. Kendall, and Mr. Dunscomb acted remarkably well. We saw Mr. Gladstone there incognito.

26th.—Drove to the railway-station, and left at 11 A.M. for Elveden Hall. We met Colonel Oliphant at Thetford station, and thence drove to Elveden Hall in Maharajah Dhuleep Sing's carriage. I was received by the Maharajah at the entrance. He introduced me to the Maharanee and children. Took a walk with the Maharajah in his park in the evening. At night took some champagne and peaches with the Maharajah and party. We saw a great many kinds of birds in the Maharajah's park.

27th.—With the Maharajah and Captain West went out shooting in the morning. We had very good sport. We got upwards of fifty head. I shot some pheasants. Returned to the house at 3 P.M. The Maharajah's house is a large and beautiful building. It is in the

DIARY OF THE RAJAH OF KOLHAPOOR.

European as well as the Oriental fashion. It has got a very large and pretty park about it. The Maharajah and Maharanee gave me a very good reception, and were very kind to me. I took leave of them at 5.30 P.M., and drove to Thetford, which we left at 6 P.M. Arrived in London at 9.30 P.M.

28*th*.—Drove in the afternoon and called on the Bishop of Madras, but he was not in the house. In the evening went to the Holborn Theatre. I liked the circus. The horses must be very carefully, and with great trouble, trained. Two men performed athletic exercises wonderfully well, and two boys also exercised very well. There were two men who exercised on horseback well, and jumped over six horses.

29*th*.—Drove in the afternoon to Aldebert's, to see our carriages. Returned at about 5 P.M.

30*th*.—Went to Stafford House to pay my respects to the Prince and Princess of Wales. They gave me a very warm reception. The Princess is a charming person; she has got a very sweet face and graceful manner. The Prince talked with me for a quarter of an hour. He is a very courteous man. Both of them talked with me very kindly. I presented a jewelled dagger to the Prince. He and the Princess were very much pleased with it. They gave me their likenesses with their autographs. Before we saw the Prince and

DIARY OF THE RAJAH OF KOLHAPOOR.

Princess the Private Secretary of the former met me in a room, in which we had an audience of the former. Stafford House is a large, fine building, and is beautifully furnished. We then took a drive and returned home.

31st.—Drove to the Horse Guards at 11 A.M. and saw how the Guards are changed. Afterwards to the Victoria Station, and left for Beckenham at 11.30. At the Station of Beckenham Captain W—— with his Maxy met us. Then we drove to Mr. M——'s, where we said good-by to him and his family. Took some champagne and grapes there. I cannot help remarking here that Mr. and Mrs. M—— have been very kind and hospitable to me since my arrival in England. They are good, kind-hearted people in my opinion. Mr. D. M—— is a jolly and amiable man. I have got a great regard for the M——'s.

Arrived at Victoria Station at 2.20. Drove to Lady F——'s party in Prince's Gardens. Lady and Sir B. F—— introduced me to several European and native ladies and gentlemen. All the F——'s gave me a very warm reception and were very kind to me. I need not write here about Sir B. F—— and all his family being exceedingly kind and hospitable to me whenever I met them.

1st November.—Drove to Victoria Station with Captain West and all my men, and left for Dover at 7.45. Arrived at 10.30 A.M.

DIARY OF THE RAJAH OF KOLHAPOOR.

Passed through a beautiful country. Left Dover at 11 A.M. and sailed to Ostend, where we arrived a little after 3 P.M. I was very sea-sick. The sea was very rough. Stayed in an hotel at Ostend till 5.45 P.M. and took our luncheon there. Left at 6.30, and arrived at Brussels at 9.30 P.M. Drove to the "Hotel de Flandre," which is a large and fine building. I felt leaving England.

2nd.—Mr. J. Saville Lumley, English Ambassador at the Belgian Court, called on me at 12.30. In the afternoon drove through the principal parts of the city, and then went to the Town Hall, which is a large fine carved stone building. There are many rooms in which beautiful tapestry is hung up, and some fine pictures of the Kings of Belgium are hung up also. There is a large fine carved room in which the Municipal Council is held, and there is a room for civil marriages also. Then we drove to the Court of Justice, in which two beautiful pictures are hung up— one in which Charles V., Emperor of Germany, Belgium, Netherlands, &c., gave up the crown, and the other in which a document agreed to by the noblemen was signed by one of them on behalf of Philip II.* After taking a drive to the City, went to the cathedral, which is a beautiful large carved building. It is seven

---

* The Rajah evidently did not quite comprehend the explanation given to him of the famous "Compromise of the Nobles."—ED.

DIARY OF THE RAJAH OF KOLHAPOOR.

hundred years old, and it has got fine stained glass windows. There is also a beautifully carved pulpit. Returned to our hotel at 5.30. Brussels is a fine clean city. It has got broad streets and very fine buildings.

3rd.—Drove at 11 A.M. to see the battle-field of Waterloo. Saw the two principal points at which the French made several attacks on the English. The Château of Hougoumont and La Haye Sainte are the above points. There is a tower near the latter place on the top of which there is a bronze statue of a lion. From this place we got a very good view of the different positions of both the armies. Napoleon was during the whole battle at a place called La Belle Alliance, and here the Duke of Wellington and Prince Blucher met each other. We went first to a church where the leg of the Marquis of Anglesea was buried and some other officers were interred also. There is a house near it where Wellington passed the night before the battle. I am very glad that I have seen Waterloo. I took my luncheon in a house near the tower. There is a small museum near the tower in which a great many relics of the battle are kept by a lady whose uncle fought at Waterloo. I bought some of the relics and some books connected with the battle of Waterloo. We have enjoyed our trip to Waterloo very much. Returned to our hotel about 6 P.M.

DIARY OF THE RAJAH OF KOLHAPOOR.

4th.—Went to the old and modern picture galleries at 11 A.M. and saw some beautiful and valuable pictures and statues. There are very good collections of pictures and statues in both these museums. The buildings are very fine also. Afterwards, with Captain West and a General sent by the King to conduct me to his palace, drove in the King's very beautiful and gorgeous carriage to see the King of the Belgians. I was received at the entrance of the palace by some of the officers of the King, and at the top of the staircase by others. The English Envoy met me upstairs also. The King shook hands with me and spoke very politely and gently with me for more than a quarter of an hour. He has been to India; therefore the general talk was about it. The King gave me, in short, a very warm and kind reception and was exceedingly polite to me. He came with me as far as the top of the staircase. Then I was conducted by the English Ambassador and some of the King's officers to the carriage. With the same General and in the same carriage we returned to the hotel at 2 P.M. The King is a tall, handsome man, and he is very polite and gentle in his manners. Called on the English Envoy at 3 P.M. and drove to the Duke of Aremberg's palace, where we saw some beautiful pictures and a very nice library. The picture gallery and the palace are beautiful.

DIARY OF THE RAJAH OF KOLHAPOOR.

In the evening, with Captain West, a King's general, and an aide-de-camp, drove in the King's carriage to see the opera. The English Envoy joined us there. The opera-house is very pretty, and the King's box and the whole house are nicely furnished. We took some champagne in the refreshment-room, and returned to the hotel at 10 P.M. I could not understand the play as it was in French.

The Belgians are noted for farming, and they appear to be quiet and frugal.

5th.—Went to the station at 9 A.M. and left for Cologne at 10 A.M. Arrived at Cologne at about 5 P.M. Drove immediately to the "Hotel de Belle Vue." It is a good hotel and commands a very good view of the Rhine which flows beside it. The arrangements in the hotel are said to be good and perfect.

6th.—In the morning, took a drive through the principal parts of the city. Saw a great many French prisoners in the streets. Then we went to the cathedral which is a beautiful large carved building. It has very pretty stained glass windows. It is about six hundred years old. There is a silver shrine in it. Then we drove to the museum which contains some beautiful pictures and busts. Cologne is a fortified and curious-looking town. It is full of the French prisoners at present. There are earth fortifications in front of the

DIARY OF THE RAJAH OF KOLHAPOOR.

stone walls. The Rhine is very broad and it has got fresh water. There are two bridges on the Rhine near Cologne—one is of boats and the other of solid iron. The latter is very nice and strong. It must have cost very largely. Germans are celebrated for learning and smoking. Every German must learn military tactics. It is a rule that every German should be for a certain time in the army.

7th.—Drove to the station at 4.45 P.M. and left at 5 P.M. for Frankfort, where we arrived at 10.30 P.M. We are staying here in the "Hotel de Russie." It is a very nice hotel and is beautifully furnished. Our drawing-room and bed-rooms are like staterooms. I was poorly this morning.

8th.—Drove in the forenoon to the Town Hall, in which there are pictures of the Emperors of Germany from the earliest date. Then we drove to a church in which the Emperors used to be crowned, and there is a room in which they were elected. In it there is a chair lined with red velvet on which they were crowned. This is a large church. Thence we drove to a picture gallery where we saw some fine pictures and busts. Took a drive through the principal parts of the city. Passed through the Jewish street and saw their synagogue and the house belonging to the predecessors of the Baron Rothschild. Frankfort is a large, old-looking town, and it is built in the old fashion.

DIARY OF THE RAJAH OF KOLHAPOOR.

9th.—Drove to the station and left for Munich at 10.40 A.M. Arrived at 9.45 P.M. I was very much tired by such a long journey. Some part of the country through which we passed was beautiful. We are staying in the "Hotel of the Four Seasons," which is a good one. The rooms in it are nicely furnished.

10th.—In the forenoon went first to the picture gallery, which contains many beautiful paintings painted by celebrated artists. Then we went to see the statue of Bavaria which is a colossal one. There is a lion near it. The whole statue is of bronze. The top of it can hold eight men. I have never seen such a large statue before. Took a drive through the principal parts of the city and the park. Munich is a nice large city. It has got beautiful buildings. It is the capital of Bavaria.

11th.—Went first to the Royal Palace at 11 A.M. The palace is a large and beautiful stone building. The state-rooms are very nicely and richly ornamented and furnished. As we could not find our carriage we were obliged to return to our hotel in a cab. Afterwards went to the library, which contains 800,000 volumes, and some very interesting Oriental as well as European MSS. and pictures of different tribes. It is a large building and it has got a very large and broad staircase at the entrance. Then we went and saw a cathedral and a church. Both of them are large, beautiful brick buildings. They are nearly four hundred years old. Then we drove to the National Museum, which is also a large building, and which contains many kinds of arms and armour, machines of torture, embroidered and gorgeous ladies' and gentlemen's dresses, beautiful carved ironwork, &c. Returned to our hotel about 2 P.M. To-day is the first time I have seen snow falling.*

12th.—Leaving Munich at 10 A.M., arrived at Innsbruck at 6 P.M. The scenery was exceedingly beautiful, especially in the Tyrol. Everything was covered with snow. Changed carriages twice. Stayed at the "Hotel d'Autriche,"—good and comfortable.

13th.—At twelve drove to see the Cathedral at Innsbruck. It contains the tomb of Maximilian I. and monuments to the memory of a great many kings and queens; also one to André Hofer, a Tyrolese patriot. We then drove to the Castle Amras,† which contains a great many pictures and cabinets. It contains also the portrait of Philippina, considered the most beautiful lady of her time. It commands a charming view of Innsbruck and the adjoining country. Snow all round. Then, after a drive through the city, returned about 2 P.M. In the evening I had an attack of fever and was very poorly.

---

* This is the last entry in the Rajah's handwriting in the original Diary. The few entries that follow were written from his dictation.—ED.

† The Chateau d'Ambras.—ED.

DIARY OF THE RAJAH OF KOLHAPOOR.

14th.—A little better, but could not walk on account of a slight attack of rheumatism.

15th.—Much better but still could not walk.

16th.—Could not walk; was therefore carried on a chair to the carriage which took me to the station. At the station I was carried from the carriage to the railway carriage by three or four of my men. Left Innsbruck at 9.30 A.M. We passed through a lovely mountainous country, rich in grand and imposing scenery, especially at the Brenner Pass. Arrived at Botzen at 3 P.M. Was carried to my room from the carriage that took me from the station. The hotel is called "Kaiserkrone." A European doctor advised me to rub some ointment on my feet.

The illness mentioned in the concluding lines of the Rajah's Diary did not at first seem sufficiently serious to cause any alarm. The rheumatism, it is true, deprived him of the use of his legs, but he suffered little pain, and appeared, in other respects tolerably well. He declined the attendance of any medical man but the Mahomedan physician who had accompanied him from India, and for several days seemed to be making some, though slow, progress

DIARY OF THE RAJAH OF KOLHAPOOR.

towards recovery. In Venice, he was well enough to be carried in a sedan chair to see the Palace of the Doges and the Piazza di San Marco, and it was not till the arrival of the party in Florence that the plan of going *via* Rome and Naples to Brindisi was given up. At Florence the Rajah was induced to consult an English physician, under whose treatment he seemed to be getting on well. A change for the worse, however, suddenly came on. Two of the leading Italian practitioners were called into consultation by Dr. Fraser, and for a time the patient appeared to rally, but on the morning of the 30th November he suddenly expired. The cause of his death was stated to be "congestion of the abdominal viscera, together with collapse of nervous power."

The question of the disposal of the Rajah's remains after his death gave rise to some difficulties. His Hindoo attendants shrank from the idea of the body being embalmed or disposed of in any way but that prescribed by their religion, namely, cremation. On the other hand, cremation, except in the case of Shelley, had not been heard of in Italy for centuries, and the municipal law of Florence ordained, under penalty of two years' imprisonment, that whenever any one died the corpse should be buried in a coffin. Through the kind and untiring exertions, however, of Sir Augustus Paget, the British Minister, and Signor Peruzzi, the Syndic of

DIARY OF THE RAJAH OF KOLHAPOOR.

Florence, who laid the matter before one official after another, and finally brought it before the Council of Ministers, all difficulties were at last overcome, and the requisite permission granted. On the morning of the 1st December, a little more than twenty-four hours after his death, the remains of the Rajah were burnt by his attendants on a pyre erected on the banks of the Arno, a short distance beyond the Cascini; and it was no small consolation to them that they had thus been enabled to dispose of their prince's body according to the rites of their religion. The official *procès verbal* describing the ceremony, drawn up by the Florentine authorities, is given in the Appendix.

On the very day of the Rajah's death the sad news was received by telegraph in Kolhapoor, and caused the most profound grief in the palace and throughout the state. Of the two widows left by his Highness one was a child, but the other had lived with her husband and borne him a daughter, who, however, survived her birth but a few weeks. The grief of this lady may be imagined, as also that of the Rajah's adoptive mother, and of his cousins, who had always been brought up with him, and whom he regarded as his brother and sister. In the town, too, and throughout the territory, genuine sorrow was universally displayed. A public meeting to subscribe for a memorial of the deceased prince was

DIARY OF THE RAJAH OF KOLHAPOOR.

held in Kolhapoor, which was attended by all the influential people of that part of the country, and among them some neighbouring chiefs of a family that had for upwards of a century been at deadly feud with the Kolhapoor dynasty, but who had learned to regard the Rajah with respect and affection. The resolutions passed by this meeting, as also those passed at one held in Bombay for a similar purpose, will be found in the Appendix.

But it was not in Kolhapoor only that sincere regret was felt for the Rajah's untimely end. His name had now become known far beyond the limits of his own territory, and there were few people caring for India who did not watch his career with interest, and mourn for its premature close as for a national calamity. Some regretted the event on merely public grounds—lamenting that India had been deprived of a prince of such culture and promise, who had already set such a bright example to his countrymen, and fearing that his death under such circumstances would deter natives of rank from visiting Europe, especially when taken in connection with the decease of the Rajah of Kuppurthulla while *en route* to England. Those, however, who had been brought into contact with the late Rajah, while fully alive to the loss sustained by the public, had their regret enhanced by a feeling of warm personal regard for the deceased. No one met him without having a kindly feeling towards

DIARY OF THE RAJAH OF KOLHAPOOR.

him, and the favourable impression he left, and the golden opinions he won in England have recently been dwelt upon by Mr. Grant Duff, the Under Secretary of State for India, in his place in the House of Commons.

The writer may be permitted to add that no one knew the Rajah better or mourned for him more sincerely than the officer who had been appointed to act as his governor, and whose special charge he had been for nearly four years. Captain West, as has been mentioned, accompanied his Highness to Europe, was continually with him while there, and watched with the most intense interest the effects of the visit on the Rajah's mind. What these effects were may be gathered to some extent from the pages of the preceding Diary, but the Rajah was not given enough to reflection and analysis to be enabled to note mental phases and changes. Some things he did note; for instance, he wrote to a friend in India, not long after his arrival in England, that he had learned one thing—what a very insignificant person the Rajah of Kolhapoor was out of his own territory. This statement was made simply and without humiliation, being merely the result of enlarged powers of mental and moral perspective. But the Rajah gained much more than this knowledge. Seeing Englishmen in their best aspect—at home; seeing their institutions flourishing, not with the thin

DIARY OF THE RAJAH OF KOLHAPOOR.

weedy growth of exotics, but with all the hardy vigour of native plants; sitting at their tables, and living among and with them in a way that had been unheard of in India (though he declared his intention of adhering to the same habits on his return); brought into contact with Royalty, which he regarded with profound veneration —a veneration not diminished by the contact—the mind of the Rajah was deeply impressed by what he saw and heard around him. It was somewhat of a shock to him, perhaps, at first, to see the Prime Minister of England and Her Majesty's Principal Secretary of State for India walking quietly to a railway station, *en route* to the Presence, with umbrellas in their hands, and no retinue, but he soon learned that ostentatious display is not necessary for dignity. The softening and increased refinement of his manners were remarked by all who observed him closely, and he imbibed, what was indeed congenial to his amiable character, a feeling of consideration for others that had not previously been remarked in him.

He had always had liberal and enlightened ideas on the subject of the emancipation of the female sex from the bondage it labours under in India, but he held these ideas far more practically, and with far greater vigour after his visit to England. One of his last acts in that country was to make arrangements for engaging a lady to come out for the purpose of training and educating the ladies of

DIARY OF THE RAJAH OF KOLHAPOOR.

his family, whom he declared his intention of introducing into society as soon as they were qualified to move in it. It is not necessary to go into further detail here. The effect on the Rajah's mind of his visit to Europe may be summed up thus—he became more attached to the English and more alive to their good qualities. Without losing a particle of affection for his own country and people, he saw more clearly what was lacking in them, and determined, as far as in him lay, to labour for the improvement of both. It may be added that he enjoyed his visit so much that he fully determined to repeat it.

The honours paid to the memory of the late Rajah by the public at Kolhapoor and Bombay have been alluded to above, and the notice taken by the authorities of the sad event must not be omitted. On the 1st December, 1870, the day after the Rajah's death, the following Extraordinary Gazette was published by the Bombay Government :—

POLITICAL DEPARTMENT.
NOTIFICATION.
Bombay Castle, 1st December, 1870.

His Excellency the Right Honourable the Governor in Council announces with deep regret the receipt of intelligence of the death of his Highness

DIARY OF THE RAJAH OF KOLHAPOOR.

RAJARAM MAHARAJ CHUTRUPUTTEE, the Rajah of Kolhapoor, which melancholy event occurred at Florence, on the 30th ultimo.

The many amiable qualities of his Highness, his intelligence, and the desire he evinced to devote himself to secure the welfare of the people whom he was so soon to be called on to govern, render his premature removal the greater loss both to his subjects and the Government. It is hereby directed, as a mark of respect to the memory of the deceased Prince, that twenty minute guns, corresponding with the age of his Highness, be fired from the Saluting Battery.

By order of the Right Honourable the Governor in Council.

(Signed) W. WEDDERBURN,
Acting Secretary to Government.

The Viceroy also telegraphed his condolences, which were duly conveyed to the family in Durbar. Nothing, however, gave so much gratification as the following letter, written to the Dowager Ranee, the late Rajah's adoptive mother, by the Queen's gracious command :—

India Office, 5th January, 1871.

MY ESTEEMED FRIEND,—

I HAVE received her Majesty's commands to communicate to your Highness the deep regret and concern with which the Queen has been made acquainted with the lamentable event which has deprived you of your son, his Highness the Rajah of Kolhapoor. It had afforded her Majesty great pleasure to welcome him on his visit to England, and she had hoped

DIARY OF THE RAJAH OF KOLHAPOOR.

that on his return to India she should receive from time to time the welcome intelligence of your son's continued health and prosperity, and tidings of his benevolent efforts to improve the administration of the important country committed to his care. But it has pleased the Almighty Disposer of events to decree it otherwise, and all have learnt with the deepest sorrow that an amiable and promising Prince, who might have rendered important services to his countrymen and been an example to future rulers, has been cut off in the flower of his youth, before he could return to his native country and take the reins of government into his hands. On your Highness the blow must have fallen heavily indeed, and I am to assure you that no one more sincerely sympathises with you in your bereavement than her Most Gracious Majesty the Queen.

Offering your Highness, on my own part, the warmest expressions of my condolence on this melancholy occasion,

I am your Highness'
Sincere friend and well-wisher,

Her Highness Ahilya Bace Sahib,   (Signed)   ARGYLL.
of Kolapore.

The Rajah having left no son, the question of succession to the State of Kolhapoor is under consideration at present by Government. The result will probably be known before these pages are published.

EDWARD W. WEST.

Kolhapoor, 8th June, 1871.

DIARY OF THE RAJAH OF KOLHAPOOR.

POSTSCRIPT.

SINCE the above pages went to press the question of succession to the Kolhapoor principality has received a solution, and the throne is no longer vacant. The Political Agent was directed some time ago to ascertain the wishes of the family as to the person to be made by adoption son and heir to the late Rajah. The choice was of course limited to the collateral descendants of the Great Sivajee; but, as these are somewhat numerous, the consideration of their various claims and qualifications was a matter of no little difficulty. At last, however, the members of the royal family who were consulted unanimously recommended that Narrain Rao, son of Dinkur Rao Bhonslay—a man of some standing in the Kolhapoor State—should be adopted. The reasons that determined this selection were—that the boy in question, besides being physically and, as far as could be judged, mentally superior to most of the

DIARY OF THE RAJAH OF KOLHAPOOR.

other claimants, was the nearest in collateral descent to the main line of Sivajee, and belonged to the branch of the family from which a former Rajah of Kolhapoor had been selected and adopted. This recommendation was approved by the Bombay Government, and was sent on for the approval of the Government of India, whose sanction was accorded in time to enable the adoption to take place at the Dussera : — the great religious festival of the Mahrattas, who consider it a peculiarly auspicious time for the commencement of any undertakings, and who, in days of yore, always looked on it as the beginning of the campaigning season.

Accordingly, on the 23rd October, 1871, the adoption was solemnly performed at the palace in the presence of the Political Agent, his assistants, and all the leading chiefs and officials of the Kolhapoor State, with all due ceremonies; the boy's father making him over, with symbolical pouring forth of water, to Tara Bace,* the senior widow of the late Rajah, who took him in her lap, thereby receiving him as her husband's child, after which she proceeded with him before the family god, where the rites prescribed by the Hindoo ritual were duly performed. The new Rajah received at his adoption the name of Sivajee, and,

---

* Senior, that is, in position, as being first-married, for she is some years younger than the second Ranee.

DIARY OF THE RAJAH OF KOLHAPOOR.

after the religious ceremonies were over, was placed on a *gadee* or cushion, where the leading chiefs of the state rendered homage to him, and laid at his feet the customary presents. In the evening he was received, with the honours due to his rank, at a Durbar held at the Residency, and his name and dignity were formally announced to those there assembled.

The young Rajah, who is but eight and a half years old, shows fair promise even at that early age. His face is intelligent and pleasing, especially when he smiles, and it is hoped that with the careful training and education which he will receive his mind and better qualities will be so developed that he will prove worthy to succeed the accomplished and amiable Prince whose son he has now become.

APPENDIX.

I. The Durbar at Poona in 1866.
II. The Durbar at Poona in 1868.
III. The Ceremony of Laying the Foundation-Stone of the High School at Kolhapoor.
IV. The *Procès-verbal* of the Cremation at Florence.
V. Resolutions passed by a Public Meeting assembled at Kolhapoor to do Honour to the Memory of the late Rajah.
VI. Resolutions passed by a Public Meeting assembled at Bombay for the Same Purpose.
VII. A Brief Account of the Ceremonies attending the Adoption of a Successor to the Kolhapoor Gadee.

APPENDIX.

I.

THE DURBAR AT POONA IN 1866.

(From the Official Account.)

HIS EXCELLENCY SIR HENRY BARTLE EDWARD FRERE, G.C.S.I. and K.C.B., Governor of Bombay, held a Durbar at Poona on the 29th October, 1866, for the reception of his Highness the Rajah of Kolhapoor, the Rajah of Jowar, the Sirdars and Chiefs of the Deccan and Southern Mahratta country, and other native gentlemen.

On the arrival of his Highness the Rajah of Kolhapoor, the guard of honour presented arms, and he was received by the Political Secretary to Government and the Political Agent, Kolhapoor and Southern Mahratta country, and was taken to his seat.

* * * * * *

These, together with the principal civil and military officers of the station, having assembled, his Excellency the Governor, accompanied by his Excellency Sir Robert Napier, K.C.B., Commander-in-Chief, entered the

APPENDIX.

Durbar, attended by his personal staff, the Secretary and Under-Secretary to Government in the Political Department, and Mr. Venayrk Wassoodew, Oriental Translator to Government, and took his seat under the usual salute.

His Excellency the Governor was supported on the left by his Excellency Sir Robert Napier, K.C.B.; the Honourable B. H. Ellis; the Honourable C. S. Erskine; his Highness Meer Hussun Ali Khan of Sind; his Highness Syud Abdool Uzeez of Muscat and Zanzibar; the Honourable the Advocate-General; the Honourable Framjee Nusserwanjee; Major-General Smith, C.B.; Brigadier-General Sir C. Staveley, K.C.B.; the heads of the Civil Departments, and the officers of the Poona Brigade and the Kirkee Station.

On the right his Excellency the Governor was supported by Mr. Lloyd, the Agent for Sirdars in the Deccan; Mr. Havelock, Collector of Tanna; Colonel Anderson, Political Agent Kolhapoor and Southern Mahratta country; Mr. Arthur, Collector of Sattara; Mr. Watt, Assistant Agent for Sirdars in the Deccan; and Captain Waller, V.C., Adjutant of the Kolhapoor Infantry and Assistant to the Political Agent.

His Highness the Rajah of Kolhapoor had a raised seat next to that of his Excellency the Governor, and his ministers and mankureers sat near him in the following order:—

1. Ramrao Nursing Tarputry.
2. Narayenrao Sahib Ghatgey Surjerao.
3. His son, Dutajeerao Aba Sahib.
4. Shreeniwass Pundit *alias* Rowjee Maharaj.
5. Krushnarao Bhaoo Sahib Punt Prutinidhee of Vishalgur.

APPENDIX.

6. Moreshwur Baba Sahib Punt Amatya of Bowra.
7. Suntajeerao Ghorepuray Senaputtee of Kapsee.
8. Govindrao Aba Sahib Ghorepuray, Chief of Inchulkurunjee.
9. Soobhanrao Sahib Senakhaskel of Torgul.
10. Gopalrao Sahib Sur Lushkur Bahadoor.
11. Narayenrao Ghorepuray Umeerool Oomrao of Dutwar.

* * * * * *

After the reception had taken place his Excellency Sir Bartle Frere addressed his Highness the Rajah of Kolhapoor, in English, as follows :—

RAJAH RAM CHUTTRAPUTTEE MAHARAJ,—

I CORDIALLY welcome your Highness to Poona, and I regard your visit as a great consolation for the grief with which the Government heard of the death of his Highness the late Rajah. Your Highness has succeeded, as his son, to a great and onerous inheritance. As the head of an ancient house so famous in Mahratta history, as the ruler of many fair provinces and of hundreds of thousands of subjects whose happiness will depend so greatly on the manner in which you rule them, you have heavy responsibilities early laid upon you, and I heartily pray that God may give you strength and wisdom to sustain them. You have, to assist you, the good example of his late Highness, and the excellent system of government already established, the aid of tried and faithful servants like Ram Row and your other ministers, and above all the constant assistance and advice of an experienced resident, Colonel George Sligo Anderson, who is already well known to you by his able services in other parts of the Southern Mahratta country, and who will, I am sure, speedily secure your

APPENDIX.

entire confidence, as he has earned that of the British Government. I would earnestly exhort you to regard him as your best friend, and to refer to him all your doubts and difficulties, whatever they may be, remembering what you have heard the State of Kolhapoor owed to Colonel Douglas Graham when your predecessor was a minor, and still later, what you have yourself seen of the confidence which existed between his late Highness and Mr. Havelock. I trust at no distant period to hear from Colonel Anderson that he considers you capable of conducting the whole administration without the intervention of a regency. But I would beg your Highness to remember that this period will be hastened or retarded according as you apply yourself to carry out the course of study so wisely laid down for you by his late Highness. It was a great source of gratification to me to learn that since I had the pleasure of seeing you at Kolhapoor, less than a year ago, you had made such progress in your studies that you wished me to address you in English, and that you were prepared to reply in the same language. I am glad to infer from this circumstance that you are fully alive to the fact that the office of ruler of Kolhapoor is no empty honour, no mere agreeable pageant, and it is certain that the British Government will not entrust the active powers of administration to any one, till they have all the security for a wise use of these powers which good education and proved disposition can afford. I would in the meantime have you constantly bear in mind that no former Rajah of Kolhapoor ever succeeded to dignities and responsibilities equal to yours. However absolute their power, it was circumscribed within a very short radius from their capital. None of them could have ventured as far as you have come from your capital without fear of domestic treachery or foreign violence. There are old men now alive who can tell you what

APPENDIX.

were the dangers in their early days of a visit from Kolhapoor to your ancestor's capital at Sattara, or to his minister's capital at Poona. But wherover your Highness now goes you move under the ægis of the British power, with no more retinue than you require for purposes of convenience or state. You can travel unarmed from Cashmere to Ceylon and no man can let or hinder you with impunity. Nay more, you may in like manner visit any civilized country in the world, in the furthest parts of Europe or America, and you will everywhere be received and protected, not merely with the hospitality due to a sovereign prince, but as one entitled to the protection of the whole power of the British Empire. And this you have obtained at no other sacrifice than that of the power to do evil with impunity. There was a time when your predecessors could exercise any amount of oppression over their subjects, and no power in India could call them to account. Such licence of oppression exists no longer. But there is nothing which a good Rajah of Kolhapoor could ever have done which you may not do now; and if the Rajah's power to do evil has been limited, his power to do good and his responsibility for the exercise of that power have been immensely increased. I know but of two conditions to the enjoyment of this power. They are fidelity to the British Crown, and the obligation to govern your subjects well. I am convinced that no exhortation of mine is needed to impress on your Highness or your advisers your responsibilities in both respects; and I draw from the example of your lamented predecessor the assurance that you will be no less anxious to deserve the character of a faithful ally to her Majesty the Sovereign of the British Empire, than to follow her example as a beneficent and beloved ruler, ever protecting the rights of all her subjects, and tempering

APPENDIX.

justice with mercy. I have now the Viceroy's permission to recognize your Highness as the adopted son of the late Rajah of Kolhapoor, and as his successor; and may God give you grace to reign long and wisely and happily over the people committed to your charge.

At the conclusion of this address a Poshak * was given to his Highness the Rajah, and a salute of seventeen guns was fired. His Highness replied in English to his Excellency the Governor as follows:—

YOUR EXCELLENCY,—

I THANK you most heartily for the kind welcome you have given me and the great honour which I have received at your Excellency's hands on this auspicious day. I beg that your Excellency will convey to her Most Gracious Majesty the assurance of my loyal devotion to her crown, and my desire to fill worthily the high position to which, by Divine Providence, I have succeeded, under the sovereign of this great Empire. I feel deeply sensible of the responsibilities which have fallen on me, and how much will be needed on my part to fulfil them in a way which will do honour to the memory of the illustrious Prince whose early loss we all deplore. The words of advice spoken by your Excellency to-day can never be effaced from my memory, and will guide and cheer me in the arduous path before me, as the words of a revered parent who has earnestly at heart the honour and happiness of the ancient house of Sivajee, and the welfare of the nobles and people attached to it. Knowing how much

---

* Set of robes of investiture.—ED.

APPENDIX.

the principality of Kolhapoor owes to the care and protection of the British Government, it will always be my duty to look to the Political Agent at my court for counsel and encouragement. I esteem myself especially fortunate in having so kind and experienced a gentleman as Colonel Anderson to advise and befriend me on entering on the duties of my high station, and I trust by God's blessing and the continued friendship and protection of the British Government, to hand down unimpaired the great inheritance to which I have this day succeeded.

*   *   *   *   *

Flowers and pansooparee having been distributed, his Excellency left the Durbar under the usual salute.

The Rajahs, Sirdars, and Chiefs were conducted to their carriages in the same manner in which they had been received.

II.
THE DURBAR AT POONA.
(From the Bombay Gazette.)

Friday, October 9, 1868.

THE first Durbar held by Sir Seymour Fitzgerald took place at Poona on Thursday. The scene of the ceremonial was the handsome hall of the Engineering College, a room well adapted for the purpose, under the circumstances. The day was fine, the roads were crowded with natives in holiday costume, and they evidently enjoyed the tumasha, as they always do. Nothing could have been more successful than the imposing ceremony, and no one could have performed his part, as representative of the Queen, better than the

APPENDIX.

Governor. The chiefs and sirdars mustered in considerable force, and several were attended by groups of followers, more or less picturesquely attired. There was a brisk demand for vehicles of all sorts: neither the elephant nor even the pulki was wanting. Outside the hall were guards of honour, both horse and foot; in the latter the British infantry were conspicuous for their solid and handsome appearance. A battery was drawn up just off the road, and suggested, like the British guards, the power that lay under the surface of the lively display.

Within the hall the native rajahs and sirdars were seated in rows on each side of the avenue leading to the dais: placed at the end opposite the door. A gold-bespangled cloth or carpet overspread the steps and the platform. Three chairs were placed thereon. That on the right was filled by the Rajah of Kolhapoor, that on the left by the Maharajah of Edur. The central seat, covered with cloth of gold, was intended for his Excellency the Governor. Further off, to the right and left, were seats for the members of the Civil Service, the Legislative Council, and the Military Staff. The galleries were originally intended for the ladies—and they formed a bright portion of the spectacle—but a pressure for space compelled several gentlemen to seek the galleries, and red and blue uniforms and black coats formed a background to the fair ladies of Poona. One portion of the gallery, screened from profane eyes by lattice-work, was set apart for the native ladies who had the courage to attend. About half-past four, the sound of guns and the strains of the band announced the arrival of the Governor, who presently walked up the avenue to his seat, amid the whole audience, who stood to receive him. He shook hands with the near neighbours of his throne, and bowing to the assembly, seated himself—a signal for the down-sitting of all. Then, one after another,

APPENDIX.

the rajahs were presented, the boy-Rajahs of Barca, Loonawarra, and Jowar, leading the way. Nuzzeranas were tendered, and presents made in return; the High Priest of the Parsees—a most noble, dignified, and wonderfully well-dressed gentleman—received a handsome gold medal. Wreaths of flowers were distributed in the usual way, duly besprinkled with scent, the perfume of which filled the hall. Not the least interesting incident was the address to the Governor, read extremely well by the Rajah of Kolhapoor, whose training reflects the greatest credit on Captain West. The reply of the Governor was worthy of his reputation as a good speaker in the most fastidious chamber in the world. He was fluent, weighty, dignified. During the delivery of his speech the scene was really beautiful. All the bright colours harmonized, and produced an effect worthy of a grander scene. On the whole, though we hear there were some complaints and mischances, the ceremony was an entire success, creditable to all who had a share in the arrangements, and who took part in the proceedings.

The official programme for the day was as follows:—

On the arrival of his Highness the Rajah of Kolhapoor, a native guard of honour of the greatest strength allowed under military rules will present arms. His Highness will be received by the Political Secretary to government, and the assistant Political Agent of Kolhapoor and Southern Mahratta country, and be taken to his seat on the dais to the right of his Excellency the Governor. H.M.'s Munkurries will take their seats to his right.

* * * * *

The chiefs and sirdars having signified their intention to present an address to his Excellency the Governor, his Highness the Rajah of Kolhapoor will read the address on behalf of the assembly.

APPENDIX.

After his Excellency has replied to the address, flowers and pansooparee will be distributed.

The Political Secretary will distribute to his Highness the Rajah of Kolhapoor and his Highness the Rajah of Edur, the Rajahs of Barea, Loonawarra, and Jowar, and all first-class sirdars and others who are entitled to the honours paid to the first class.

* * * * *

After pansooparee has been distributed, his Excellency will leave the Durbar, receiving the salutations of the chiefs, sirdars, and others, who will then be led out by the same officers who received them. Another salute will then be fired for his Excellency.

The following is the address which was read by the Rajah of Kolhapoor:—

To his Excellency the Right Honourable Sir W. R. Seymour Vesey Fitzgerald, K.C.S.I., Governor of Bombay.

RIGHT HONOURABLE SIR,—

WE, the Chiefs and Sirdars of the Deccan and of Guzerat, who have for the first time assembled in Durbar to do honour to your Excellency, as the representative of her Majesty Queen Victoria, desire to mark this auspicious occasion by requesting your Excellency to convey to the foot of the throne our humble congratulations on the recent brilliant success of her Majesty's arms in Abyssinia.

Less than a year ago, your Excellency and the Commander-in-Chief of the Bombay army were commissioned by her Majesty to equip an army, in order to obtain the release of British subjects held in captivity by the King of Abyssinia, and of envoys sent in her Majesty's name, but detained, in violation of the usages of sovereigns.

APPENDIX.

We will not now allude to the anxious labours and responsibilities that fell to your Excellency during the equipment and progress of the Expedition. Under the distinguished leadership of your Excellency's honoured colleague, Sir R. Napier, since raised by his sovereign to the dignity of a peer, that Expedition has resulted in the most rapid and complete success.

Your Excellency is aware that some of our brother chiefs offered such service as they could afford, to aid her Majesty's Government in this difficult enterprise, and it was to us a peculiar pleasure to witness that amongst the troops chosen for it were several regiments of native soldiers, most of them drawn from our own provinces. It has also gratified us to observe that both Lord Napier and your Excellency have spoken so highly of the conduct of those native troops: of their patience and endurance, and of their soldierly courage before Magdala. Not only by the common ties of race, but by the firm loyalty which unites us to the throne, we humbly claim to share in the pride and satisfaction with which the whole British Empire learned of the triumphant results of the Expedition.

We cannot conclude this address without saying how deeply sensible we are that her Majesty earnestly desires the welfare and happiness of ourselves, and of the people under our care; and it is our wish that her high desires may be more and more fulfilled throughout her Indian Empire. We gratefully remember the good counsel given to us to this end by Sir Bartle Frere, and now confidently look to your Excellency to help us in diffusing the blessings of good government in the territories held by us, under the benign sway of the Empress of India.

We remain,

Your Excellency's faithful and devoted servants.

APPENDIX.

His Excellency replied at some length to the address. He commenced (says the *Poona Observer*, in a brief note of his Excellency's remarks) by warmly expressing his great gratification at meeting them; he referred to their allusion to her Most Gracious Majesty the Queen, and declared his conviction of the deep interest which she takes in all matters relating to her Indian Empire—adding, that it was to their own efforts chiefly, as exerted in enlightening, and improving their people and their territories, to which she looked to see them brought forward upon the road to civilization; he impressed upon them the extreme value of education, earnestly exhorting them to set the example in their own families; and with reference to the Abyssinian Expedition, he seized the opportunity of paying a well-merited tribute to the indefatigable and incessant labours of those officials who, though they never left this country, contributed so greatly towards that Expedition's success—a tribute which was received with considerable applause. His Excellency went on to urge upon the sirdars the advantages of frequent visits to the head-quarters of Government; visits which would, he said, always afford him pleasure—and, among other suggestions, he advised them to establish in Poona, what, at a public school at home, is called a "school" or "dame's house," wherein the young chieftains who arrived in Poona to attend the Deccan College, could be boarded and responsibly looked after, at the same time becoming intimate one with another. His Excellency concluded with a few words in Mahratti, wherein he repeated to those sirdars who could not follow him in English, the gratification he had experienced in meeting them.

The Governor, after a brief interval, departed with the customary salute and honours. The space around the hall was for a long period an animated

APPENDIX.

scene,—interested faces, bright colours, plunging horses, a mingled and moving cavalcade, all lighted up by the setting sun. It is long since Poona enjoyed such a splendid and pleasing tumasha. May there be more of them.

III.
LAYING THE FOUNDATION-STONE OF THE KOLHAPOOR HIGH SCHOOL.

THE ceremony of laying the first stone of the Kolhapoor High School building, by his Highness the Rajah of Kolhapoor, took place on the 19th of February, 1870, at 5.30 P.M., in the presence of her Highness the Dowager Ranee and other ladies of his Highness's family, the ladies and officers of the Agency and Station of Kolhapoor, many chiefs, sirdars, and officers of the State, the Masters and students of the High School and of other schools of the City of Kolhapoor, and a large concourse of people. The building has been designed by Captain Mant, R.E., in the Rajpoot style of architecture, and will provide accommodation for about 400 students. It will be on a line with, and will form a wing of, the handsome gateway leading to the Palace.

Her Highness the Dowager Ranee and party were accommodated with seats in the upper part of a small building in the vicinity, and were screened from public view. His Highness the Rajah, the Political Agent, the ladies and officers who were present, the chiefs, sirdars, and principal state officials took their seats on a platform which had been erected near the site. The ground about and the surrounding buildings were crowded with spectators, and the scene on the whole was pleasing and picturesque.

APPENDIX.

The Political Agent, Colonel G. S. A. Anderson, then rose and read the following address :—

Before your Highness proceeds to lay the first stone of this building, I would wish to make a few remarks on the subject of education in the Kolhapoor territory.

In 1844, when circumstances led to the administration being temporarily assumed by the British Government, there were no State Schools or Educational Establishments of any kind. The country was in such a condition of anarchy and disorder, and so much debt had been contracted, that the efforts of the Political Officers intrusted with the management were, of necessity, for a time principally directed to the establishment of order, good government, and financial prosperity; but from the first they were desirous, amongst other improvements and civilizing influences, of securing for the people similar advantages of education to those which had already been extended to the neighbouring British Districts. In 1848 four Vernacular Schools were opened, and, up to 1863, when his Highness the late Rajah succeeded to the government, the number had increased to eighteen, four of which, by the advice of my predecessor Mr. Havelock, were subsequently, in 1866, raised to the status of Anglo-Vernacular Schools. The aggregate attendance of pupils in these schools was latterly about 1,000.

The establishment of an English School in the City of Kolhapoor was advocated in 1850 by Mr. (now Sir Henry Lacon) Anderson, then Acting Political Superintendent, and one was opened in the following year by Major Graham. At first it was only attended by nineteen boys, but in 1866, when

APPENDIX.

the establishment of the present High School was under consideration, the number had increased to ninety-eight.

A school for the training of young sirdars was opened in the City of Kolhapoor in 1863. The attendance appears to have varied much. At one time there were as many as twenty-four boys on the school-roll, but in 1866, when the late Director of Public Instruction inspected it, only nine were present.

A Girls' School was also opened in the City in 1854, by the then Political Superintendent, Lieutenant Colonel (now Major General Sir George) Malcolm, but it appears to have fallen off after a time, and, when visited by Sir Alexander Grant in 1866, he found that it had almost ceased to exist.

In 1866, in consequence of the lamented death of your father and of your Highness's minority, the administration again devolved on the British Government, and it became my pleasant duty, as the Political Officer intrusted with the management of State affairs, to continue and extend the educational measures which had been originated by my predecessors, and if my efforts have been attended with a greater measure of success than theirs, it is because the circumstances of the present day have been very much more favourable than those of earlier times.

The State had formerly laboured under a very heavy burden of debt, and money was not forthcoming for the futherance of many works of improvement which otherwise might, and no doubt would, have been carried out; but, owing to the excellent management of the several British Officers who had conducted the administration, and also of his Highness the late Rajah, the State was entirely cleared of debt, and when I became connected

APPENDIX.

with its affairs an era of financial prosperity, previously unexampled in its annals, had commenced. The spirit of the times was also more favourable to the spread of education. Within the State itself, both amongst the members of your Royal House, and amongst the people generally, a strong feeling existed that more required to be done. I was also aware that Government took a warm interest in the matter. The late Governor, Sir Bartle Frere, always a liberal patron of education, personally assured me of his support, and the late Director of Public Instruction, Sir Alexander Grant, offered his valuable co-operation and assistance. The present Director, Mr. Peile, takes an equally warm interest in Kolhapoor educational matters.

As regards the Vernacular and Anglo-Vernacular Schools, one great object was to place them under efficient superintendence. By the advice of Sir Alexander Grant an English-speaking Deputy Educational Inspector was appointed for Kolhapoor, and the State has been extremely fortunate in securing the services of such an efficient officer as Mr. Bal Purushram Pundit. It also appeared to me essentially necessary that good teachers should be provided, and, even at the risk of being considered lukewarm in the matter, I determined not to open a single additional school until I could make sure that it would be properly conducted. I had also previously experienced the greatest difficulties in securing for other native states good teachers from British districts. I therefore determined to establish a training school for teachers, and, thanks to the exertions of Mr. Bal Purushram and the masters selected by him, the Kolhapoor State and some neighbouring districts are now being supplied with a well-instructed staff of school-teachers. There are now within the State and its dependencies thirty-two Anglo-Vernacular and Vernacular schools, with an aggregate

APPENDIX.

attendance, at the end of December last, of nearly 2,000 scholars. The present number of pupils in the training school is fifty-six, and as the education of many of them is nearly completed, I hope that about twenty additional Vernacular Schools may be opened this year, and a larger number next year. In addition to the masters supplied from the training school for the Kolhapoor State, seven have been supplied for other districts.

The support of these schools, which could be immediately increased to upwards of 100 with advantage were the services of a sufficient number of masters available, will be mainly provided for from the educational portion of the local cess, now being imposed in connection with the Revenue Survey operations in progress. As yet every school that has been opened has at once secured a good attendance, and many villages are petitioning for schools.

As regards English education, the school already established did not appear to provide sufficiently for the wants of the locality. The City of Kolhapoor contains a population of about 50,000, with a large proportion of sirdar and other families in good circumstances. There are also in the surrounding districts a number of towns containing a large sprinkling of Brahmin and other inhabitants, who fully appreciate the advantages of education. Under the circumstances, Sir A. Grant considered, and I fully coincided with him, that it would be advisable to establish a second grade High School. Accordingly one was opened in the month of June 1867, and the State was again most fortunate in securing the services of a most zealous and efficient officer in the present Head Master. Ably conducted as it is by Mr. Mahadeo Moreshwar· Kunte, and under the direct educational supervision of the Director of Public Instruction, the

APPENDIX.

school has, as yet, made very satisfactory progress, and I trust it will continue to prosper. At the end of last December the number of students attending it was 253. The main difficulty with which the new institution has hitherto had to struggle, namely the want of sufficient house accommodation, is about to be overcome, but I will again advert to the subject before requesting your Highness to proceed with the ceremony of the day. Time will not admit of my alluding to many other points of interest in connection with the High School, which has become so useful in affording a good education to the youth of this part of the country.

The best means of educating the chiefs and sirdars of the country had long engaged my attention, and experience had led me to conclude that they would be most benefited by being placed in the public schools, in some cases being afforded also the advice and assistance of tutors. Sir Alexander Grant coincided in my views, and it was therefore resolved to close the sirdars' school and arrange that the boys should attend the classes of the regular schools. The change has been attended with the best results. In the High school there are now eight chiefs and sirdars under tuition, amongst whom I may mention the Chief of Inchulkurunjee and your Highness's brother-in-law the Sur Lushcur Bahadoor as promising scholars. In the other state schools twenty young chiefs and sirdars, or sons of better-class parents, are under tuition ; amongst the number I may mention your Highness's cousin, the Chief of Kagul, and the little Chief of Bowra. The chiefs are also under obligations to my assistant, Captain West, who exercises a supervision over their education.

Nor has female education been neglected The Kolhapoor girls' school, with an attendance of about sixty-one, is in a very satisfactory condition.

APPENDIX.

It owes much to the kind patronage of your Highness's aunt, her Highness the late Bala Baee Aka Saheb, a lady of more than ordinary intelligence. Her daughter is now one of the most promising pupils in the school. Her Highness the Dowager Ranee, in like manner, has from the first taken a warm interest in the institution. The school has also had the advantage of being well managed by an able Committee, composed of the following members—Mr. Mahadeo Moreshwar Kunte, the head master of the High School; Mr. Jamsedjee Nowrojee Unwalla, your Highness's tutor; Mr. Bal Purushram Pundit, the Deputy Educational Inspector; Mr. Govind Amroot Ranudey, the Khasgee Karbharee, and Mr. Venayck Rughoonath Kaley, the Sudder Ameen. Above all, it owes a deep debt of gratitude to two ladies connected with the Agency, Mrs. Westropp and Mrs. West, for their kind-hearted exertions in behalf of the little girls, many of whom display much intelligence and aptitude in the acquisition of feminine accomplishments.

Another great difficulty to be overcome, especially in the City of Kolhapoor, was insufficient house accommodation. By degrees this is being obviated. About seventeen good school-houses have been constructed, or are under construction, in different parts of the State, and others will be commenced as soon as proper arrangements about them can be made. But it was more especially desirable that suitable house accommodation should be provided at an early period for the High School, and the matter at once received the attention it deserved. Unavoidable causes, however, have delayed the commencement of the building until the present time. Sir Alexander Grant recommended that Captain Charles Mant, of the Royal Engineers, who had acquired considerable experience in planning

APPENDIX.

school buildings, should be asked to prepare a design, and the suggestion was approved of by Government, but the press of other duties did not admit of that officer at once turning his attention to the matter. The site also presented peculiar difficulties. The City of Kolhapoor is so crowded that it was not an easy matter to secure a good site, and your Highness was desirous that the school should not be far distant from the Palace, and that it should be an ornamental building. This necessitated the removal of a large number of houses, and also the adoption of a special style of architecture, so that the school might accord with the handsome gateway and other buildings in the vicinity of the Palace. All preliminary difficulties having at last been successfully overcome, I have lost no time in commencing the work, and I trust that the building, of which your Highness is now about to lay the first stone, will prove a lasting ornament to your City of Kolhapoor. It is in the Hindoo Saracenic style of architecture, as developed in Rajpootana, and, by a fortuitous combination of circumstances, the Engineer officer who designed it is now on the spot to see that the work is properly carried out.

The Khasgee Karbharee, Mr. Govind Amroot Ranudoy, has been of the greatest assistance in making arrangements for the commencement and satisfactory progress of the work. Much assistance has also been rendered by Ishwar Row Nimbalcur, the head of the Lushkur Phud Establishment, and by the State Overseer, Mr. Khrishnajee Buchajee. Sergeant Overseer Rix, who is employed under Captain Mant to look after details, also appears to conduct his duties with much intelligence.

And now, as regards my own connection with these educational measures, I must repeat what I stated on a former occasion, that it is

APPENDIX.

a source of great gratification to me to know that in what I have done I have been carrying out your Highness's own wishes, and I trust that, under such a well-educated and liberal-minded ruler as your Highness promises to become, the Kolhapoor Educational Establishments will attain full development and success.

Finally, it is my earnest prayer that God's blessing may rest on the building about to be erected, and on the educational measures with which it is connected.

His Highness the Rajah then rose and replied as follows :—

COLONEL ANDERSON :—

AFTER the very interesting address which you have just delivered, it only remains for me to assure you of the pleasure it gives me to take part in this day's ceremony. Under any circumstances I should be glad to see Kolhapoor adorned with such a splendid building as that designed by Captain Mant, the foundation-stone of which we are now about to lay, and it is a source of special gratification to me that the building is to be applied to educational purposes. The time you have alluded to, when education was neglected in this territory, has gone by, I hope for ever, and the beauty of the new High School will serve to mark the high estimation in which education is now held. I am fully alive to its great importance, and you may rely on it that no efforts will be wanting on my part to spread its blessings as far as my influence extends. The details you have given show how much may be done, even in a short time, when those in authority have their heart in the work, and I trust

APPENDIX.

and believe that the impetus that has been lately given to the great cause of education will be no short-lived one, but will go on gaining every day new force, as prejudices disappear and enlightenment advances.

I feel deeply indebted to you, and those whose assistance you acknowledge, for all you have done to further education in the Kolhapoor State. Your enlightened and benevolent labours in behalf of that State will cause your name to live long in the memories of its inhabitants. Were other memorials wanting, the numerous schools you have caused to be founded, and especially this High School, which I believe will be one of the handsomest buildings in Western India, will prevent your being forgotten.

As it is now time to proceed with the ceremony for which we have assembled here, I will not trouble you with any further remarks, but will conclude by echoing your wish that God's blessing may be upon the work.

His Highness then performed the ceremony of laying the stone, the ornamental trowel, plumb, and mallet used by him on the occasion having been manufactured by Kolhapoor workmen. On the conclusion of the ceremony, the band of the Kolhapoor Infantry, which was in attendance, played the National Anthem, a salute was fired, and the Palace and Gateway were illuminated in honour of the occasion. After the distribution of presents by his Highness to the principal workmen, the usual formalities observed at the breaking up of native Durbars were gone through, and the company dispersed.

A copper box, containing several English and vernacular newspapers,

APPENDIX.

and specimens of the current coins of British India, was placed in a cavity of the stone. The stone will bear the following inscription, a copy of which, engraved on a copper plate, was also placed in the box:—

"The first stone of this building, designed by Captain Charles Mant, Royal Engineers, and intended as a High School for the City of Kolhapoor, was laid by his Highness Rajaram Chutraputtee, Maharajah of Kolhapoor, in the thirty-third year of the reign of her Majesty Queen Victoria; his Excellency the Right Honourable Earl Mayo, K.P., G.C.S.I., being at the time Viceroy and Governor-General of India; his Excellency the Right Honourable Sir William Robert Seymour Vesey FitzGerald, G.C.S.I.. Governor of Bombay; and Colonel George Sligo Alexander Anderson Political Agent at Kolhapoor, and Administrator of the affairs of the State during the minority of the Maharajah.

"A.D. 1870."

NOTE.—After the death of the Rajah this School, at the request of the Dowager Ranee, was formally designated "The Rajaram High School" in memory of his late Highness.—ED.

IV.

Florence, January 31st, 1871.

M. LE MINISTRE,—

I HAVE the honour to acknowledge the receipt of your Excellency's letter of the 24th instant, enclosing a "procès-verbal." of the ceremony of the burning of the mortal remains of the late Rajah of Kolhapoor, which the

APPENDIX.

Syndic of Florence has caused to be drawn up for the information and satisfaction of his Highness's family, and I beg to assure your Excellency that I shall lose no time in transmitting this document to her Majesty's Principal Secretary of State for India, with a view to its being forwarded to its intended destination.

In doing this it will be my agreeable duty to bear witness to the very great kindness and consideration evinced by the Syndic of Florence on the occasion in question, to the readiness with which, inspired by his well-known high and enlightened sentiments, he listened to my application, in the first instance, for permission for the suite of the deceased Prince to give effect to the rites of their religion, and to his earnest and successful efforts in overcoming the difficulties of various kinds which stood in the way of the performance of a ceremony so entirely novel in this country.

Her Majesty's Government will, I feel convinced, be duly sensible of these friendly services, but in the meantime I would request your Excellency to have the goodness to convey to the Syndic of Florence a repetition of the thanks which I had personally the honour to offer him in my own name for his obliging assistance under the circumstances in question, and I shall moreover wish to express my gratitude to the Minister of Justice and to the Prefect of Florence for the facilities which in their respective departments were accorded on the occasion alluded to.

I avail, &c.

(Signed.)   A. PAGET.

His Excellency,
   The Chevalier Visconti Venasta,
      &c. &c. &c.

APPENDIX.

Foreign Office, February 11th, 1871.

Sir,—

WITH reference to my letter of the 5th of December last, I am directed by Earl Granville to transmit to you herewith for the information of the Duke of Argyll a copy of a despatch from her Majesty's Minister at Florence, with its enclosures, in regard to the ceremony of burning the mortal remains of the late Rajah of Kolhapoor.

The Duke of Argyll will not fail to perceive the high testimony borne by Sir Augustus Paget to the conduct of the Syndic of Florence on the occasion of the ceremony in question.

I am, &c.

(Signed.) E. HAMMOND.

The Under Secretary of State,
  India Office.

No. 47.

Florence, January 31st, 1871.

My Lord,—

I HAVE the honour to transmit a copy and translation of a note from Chevalier Visconti Venasta, enclosing a copy of the "procès-verbal" of the ceremony of burning the mortal remains of the late Rajah of Kolhapoor, which has been drawn up by direction of the Syndic of Florence for the information and satisfaction of his Highness's family.

I am really unable to exaggerate the kindness and consideration evinced by the Syndic, Signor Peruzzi, on the above occasion. On my letting him know what was required he immediately came to the Legation to confer

APPENDIX.

upon the subject. He said at once that as far as it depended on his office he would give the necessary orders, and that he would do his best to endeavour to turn whatever difficulties might arise in other quarters. These difficulties, as it turned out, were not unimportant, but Signor Peruzzi, by his good will and energy, overcame them all, and finally everything was ordered in conformity with the wishes and customs of the Indians.

Signor Peruzzi acted in this circumstance in conformity with his well-known sentiments of religious tolerance, and also, I am convinced, from a desire to oblige in a case in which he believed her Majesty's Government must take interest.

I have the honour to enclose a copy of the reply, which I have returned to Signor Visconti Venasta's note, and in which I have repeated the thanks which I personally tendered to the Syndic on the occasion in question; but I am sure it would be highly gratifying to Signor Peruzzi if, in compliance with your Lordship's instructions, I should be enabled to convey to him the appreciation of her Majesty's Government for his friendly services, and I would also suggest that I shall be likewise authorised to convey their thanks to the Minister of Justice and to the Prefect of Florence.

I have, &c.

(Signed.)   A. PAGET.

The Earl Granville, K.G.,
    &c. &c. &c.

APPENDIX.

Florence, 24th January, 1871.

Signor,—

I have the honour to inform you that the Syndic of Florence, wishing to oblige the family of the Maharajah of Kolhapoor, has caused an accurate account of the ceremony performed in this city on the 1st of December last, during which the remains of the latter were burnt, to be drawn up.

Having received from the said Syndic a copy of this document, I hasten to forward it to you—herewith enclosed—and beg you to transmit it to the family of the deceased, which, perhaps, will not be sorry to possess some remembrance of the land in which the Prince's attendants were able to perform their native rites in perfect quiet.

Thanking you beforehand,

I avail, &c.

For the Ministry,

Sir A. Paget,   (Signed.)   A. Peirolion.
&c. &c.

Municipality of Florence.

Statement of the funeral procession and cremation of the corpse of his Highness the late Maharajah of Kolhapoor.

On the 1st December, 1870, at 1 a.m., in Florence, and precisely in the Hôtel della Pace in Manin Square, the undersigned, the Director of the Municipal Police and the Secretary of the Municipal Sanitary Commission, assisted by Signor Pier Sarruzo Ciatti, communal employé (as interpreter) by order of the Mayor, appeared to arrange, on behalf of the charge entrusted to them, about the funeral procession and subsequent cremation of the body

APPENDIX.

of his Highness the Rajah Maharajah of Kolhapoor, whose death occurred twenty-four hours previously, and was duly ascertained on the previous morning by Doctor Enrico Passigli, doctor of medicine, officiating doctor of the town for S. Luce's district.

It is known that, according to the rite of Brahma, the Prince was allowed to expire on a carpet spread for the purpose on the flooring of the room; that the formal ceremonies preceding the procession are unknown, the dignitaries of the deceased and his followers having officiated with closed doors; that it was assumed that the body had been bathed, and perhaps sprinkled with naphtha.

The superior political and civil authorities, according to the English Minister's requests, and on the advice of the Sanitarial Department, allowed that the corpse be burned according to the Indian ritual. The place chosen for the purpose was the extreme point of the Cascini (park), on the bank of the river Arno, in a deserted and open esplanade. The Indians, not having succeeded in procuring at once a perfectly new palanquin to be able to transport it with the arms, and to avoid the crowding of the curious public, an omnibus, belonging to the hotel, was made use of, in which the party held up on their knees, during the whole way, the four corners of the plank on which the corpse was deposited. The omnibus was followed by a coach, in which was Captain West, Aide-de-camp and Governor of the Prince, the undersigned, and the interpreter. Notwithstanding the early hour, and the bad weather, a number of other carriages and a numerous crowd followed the cortège. Close to the place where the funeral pile was erected, one of the Indian followers broke a black earthen vessel.

The body was conveyed by hands to the place where the rectangular-

APPENDIX.

shaped pile was raised, and provisionally deposited behind the same in the vicinity of the river.

The feeble light shown by small paper lanterns borne by the deceased's servants aided to conceal from the curious the sprinkling of the corpse and other ceremonies, the description of which is found in books on oriental customs.

At about 1.30 A.M. the body was deposited on the funeral pile (about three feet high) with the face carefully shaved, uncovered, and turned to the east. The hand litter on which the deceased was lying was thrown into the river, and abandoned to the current.

The richness of the ornaments and dresses covering the deceased was remarkable, and, among others, a necklace of large pearls, gold bracelets, and costly buckle on the turban, and sundry other jewels on the crest.* The logs were, according to the oriental custom, crossed and folded on the body; the same with the arms. The exterior coverings consisted in a rich red ground shawl with large borders embroidered with gold. The familiars then began to heap the firewood on the sides so as not to surpass the level of the corpse, whilst the Brahmin † anointed the face with ghee, camphor, sandal, and other perfumes, as well as introducing into the mouth some golden coin, and betel leaves. Among the pieces of firewood we saw thrown some kind of small mud-balls, kneeded with flour and aromatic combustible substances; the pile rising cupola-shape, concealing in the middle the body covered over with birch-trees anointed with odoriferous rosins.

---

* This is a mistake. The only articles of any value on the corpse were the shawls mentioned further on.—ED.

† There was no Brahmin with the party.—ED.

APPENDIX.

A little before 2 o'clock one of the dignitaries, provided with a perfumed torch lit at one of the paper lamps, averting his face, put fire to the top, and northern angle of the pile, letting fall at the same time a white earthen vase in the shape of a cone, which, according to the rite, should contain water from the river.

A strong north wind favoured the burning of the pile, during which the Indians were sitting down, in oriental style, and alternately praying in a low voice, and bowing respectfully towards the pile; looking at it through the left hand fingers, and handing one another a kind of white turban previously held by the Brahmin. The Hindoo * doctor of the followers shared in the ceremony.

* * * * *

Towards 10 o'clock the cremation was completed. The Hindoos remained free from the curious spectators, and almost exclusively escorted by the guards of the municipality. Then some of the escort, taking some water from the river, besprinkled the residue of the pile, and, carefully groping among the ashes, collected the fragments of bones which had escaped the action of the fire, and deposited them from hand to hand, with pious care, in a porcelain vase, which was covered with a red cloth, and packed and sealed with sealing-wax.

It is known that such residues, according to their rite, must be thrown in the sacred water of the river Ganges.† The party, after having carefully gathered the remaining ashes, cleaned and washed all round the ground, and, collecting them in a kind of sheet, brought it into the middle of

---

* The native doctor was a Mahomedan.—ED.

† This was done on the return of the party to India.—ED.

APPENDIX.

the river to be shaken into the current; making afterwards, with the mud of the Arno, the form of a heart in the centre of the space occupied by the pile, they buried some small vases containing raw and boiled rice and peas, sandalwood and betel, surmounted by small yellow banners; they also scattered copiously on the meadow a quantity of rice and peas, offered, according to the rite, to the deceased kinsman's soul, which they believe to continue wandering for some days near the place where the body was burnt. After repeated rubbing with water collected in the palm of the hand, they closed in a circle in the middle of the meadow, muttering as the custom of Mahomedans is, and bursting all out into a flood of tears, chanting some kind of funeral songs interrupted by clamours and lamentations. Rising again after a moment they took up the urn containing their master's remains, returned to the hotel, where, with pious conceit, they purchased all the furniture * used by the late prince, and those employed after his death, including the omnibus. Thus ended the funeral ceremony.

The Director of the Municipal police,
(Signed.)   LEOPOLDO.
The Secretary of the Sanitary Commission,

The Interpreter,   (Signed.)   D. AMERIGO BERGIOTTE.
(Signed.)   PIER SARRUZO CIATTI.

Vero of the Town Officer,
(Signed.)   BRANDIMARTI LALETTE.

---

* This is a mistake, possibly arising from the fact that an enormous charge was made by the hotel-keeper, on the plea that he would have to refurnish the rooms. No furniture or article was purchased by the Rajah's party.—ED.

APPENDIX.

V.

AT a numerously attended public meeting held at Kolhapoor on the 18th of December, 1870, the Chief of Jumkhundee being in the chair, to give expression to the general sense of the loss sustained by the untimely death of his Highness Rajaram Chutraputtee of Kolhapoor, and to perpetuate his memory by some suitable and lasting memorial, it was resolved—

That a letter of condolence be addressed to the mother of the late Rajah.

That certain gentlemen be appointed to act on the "Rajaram Chutraputtee Memorial Committee."

That a subscription list be opened for the purpose of endowing scholarships, to be awarded to the most deserving of the poor students attending the Kolhapoor High School. The details to be settled by the Political Agent and the Director of Public Instruction.

That the fund thus raised be called "The Rajaram Maharajah Chutraputee Memorial Fund."

A sum equivalent to about 800l. was subscribed on the spot, and the total amount collected now exceeds 2,000l.

VI.

RESOLUTIONS PASSED BY A PUBLIC MEETING HELD IN BOMBAY AT THE FRAMJI COWASJI INSTITUTE.

1. THAT this meeting do record the deep and sincere sorrow which has been caused amongst all classes of the people by the sudden death of his Highness Rajaram Chutraputtee, Maharajah of Kolhapoor, whose amiable

APPENDIX.

disposition, modesty and intelligence had rendered him a worthy representative and ornament to the house of the illustrious Shiwaji; who, though young in years, had spared no pain to qualify himself for his exalted position by an assiduous study of the English language and thereby becoming conversant with modern arts and sciences and advanced ideas of government; who, to complete his education, undertook, in spite of great difficulties, a voyage to Europe (an enterprise achieved by few Hindu princes); who was expected on all sides not only to confer immense benefits on his own subjects and on the people of Maharastra in general, but also to set an example of good government to the princes of India; but who was snatched away by death just at the moment when his return home and installation on the throne of his fathers was considered by the whole country as nigh at hand, and all eyes turned to the occasion as one of national rejoicing, and this meeting reckons the sad event as a national loss.

2. That a committee, to be appointed, should be requested to make arrangements for raising in this city some memorial of the great esteem in which this virtuous, well-beloved, and educated prince was held by all, and of the deep regret which was felt at his sudden death.

3. That a letter of condolence be addressed to his Highness's mother, and the two Rances he has left behind him, expressive of the sympathy of the country with them in their unconsolable grief; and deploring his Highness's death, in the prime of youth, as a great national loss.

4. That in order to carry out the wishes of the meeting just expressed, and in order to collect subscriptions, a committee be appointed.

APPENDIX.

VII.

A BRIEF ACCOUNT OF THE CEREMONIES ATTENDING THE ADOPTION OF A SUCCESSOR TO THE KOLHAPOOR GADEE.

On the evening of the 12th October, 1871, a telegram was received by the Political Agent conveying the sanction of his Excellency the Viceroy in Council to the adoption of Narrain Rao, son of Dinkur Rao Bhoslay Sawurdékur, as son and heir to the late Rajah, agreeably to the wishes expressed by the family of the deceased Prince. The news was immediately communicated to the palace, from which the "sugar of joy" was distributed that very night throughout the town, and elsewhere, in token of delight. Letters of summons were at once issued directing the attendance of the Kolhapoor feudatory Chiefs, Sirdars, Mankurees, and leading officials at the approaching Dussera, which was fixed on as the auspicious time for the adoption to take place, and invitations to be present on the occasion were sent to the Chiefs of the Southern Mahratta Country. The giver and receiver of the child having duly fasted, by proxy, on the day preceding the adoption, and the father having been formally asked for and having formally consented to give up his son, the latter was, on the morning of the 23rd October, conducted to the palace in state, accompanied by his father. The Rajah elect was then anointed and bathed, after which the *punya wachan* ceremony was performed, by which the presence of Gunputti and the tutelary deities was invoked. The *hom*, or sacred fire, was next lighted, after which Dinkur Rao Sawurdékur signified

APPENDIX.

by pouring water on the hands of Tara Baee, the senior (*i. e.* first-married) widow of the late Rajah, that he made over his son to her. She then went through the action of *mustakawayhrana* (literally "head-smelling"), by placing her face on the boy's head at the spot where the sutures of the skull are not joined at birth—an action of mystic significance which is considered tantamount to bringing forth the child to whom it is done. After this the boy was placed in the lap of his new mother, who fed him for the first time with sugar, and the name of Sivajee was bestowed on him with the consent of all the members of the family.

This part of the ceremony was witnessed by the Political Agent and his assistants, who had come to the palace for the purpose, and who remained in the large hall with the Chief and officials of the State, and the Chiefs of Phulton and Meeruj, while the prescribed ritual was being gone through.

The Ranee and her newly-adopted son were then taken before the image of Amba Baee, in the palace, after which the boy was taken to the Dowager Ranees, each of whom repeated the ceremony of putting sugar in his mouth. On his return, his mother seated herself again with him in her lap, and the Rajah's titles were proclaimed by the Chobdars, after which he took his seat on the gadee, and received the homage and offerings of his Sirdars and Mankurees and the presents of the Chiefs of the Southern Mahratta Country, one of whom, the Chief of Meeruj, was present on the occasion. The Rajah then advanced into the body of the hall, and took his seat by the Political Agent, shortly after which pan and sooparee, &c., were distributed in the usual manner, and the Durbar broke up. The Rajah then proceeded through the crowds of mendicants, to whom alms

APPENDIX.

were being distributed in honour of the occasion, to the temple of Amba Baee.

On the evening of the same day, at five o'clock, a full-dress Durbar was held at the Residency for the reception of his Highness the Rajah, who came in state, and was received with the honours due to his rank, a guard of honour composed of one hundred men of the 17th Regiment, N. I., with the regimental colour and drums and fifes, being drawn up to salute him on his arrival and departure. The Durbar was attended by all the gentlemen of the station, together with the Sirdars and chief officials of the Kolhapoor State, to whom the Political Agent formally announced the adoption and accession of the Rajah, expressing at the same time, the pleasure it gave him to do so, and the earnest hope he entertained that his Highness would, as he grew up, follow in the footsteps of his adoptive father Rajaram Maharaj, whose loss had been so deeply lamented by all classes.

The Chief of Meeruj was at the same Durbar invested with the administration of his estate, and was presented with the poshak, or honorary dress, sent by Government to be given to him on the occasion.

On the evening of the 24th October, a grand display of fireworks took place on the bank of the Panchgunga river, where tents had been pitched and seats placed for the accommodation of the Rajah, his Sirdars, and the ladies and gentlemen of the station. The fireworks, which were admirable, were made for the occasion by some of the employés in the military department of the State, and were shown to great advantage by the position selected for the display.

The greater part of the 25th idem was spent by the State officials at

APPENDIX.

Kolhapoor in distributing alms in honour of the occasion to mendicants. About 5,000 rupees were distributed in this way to upwards of ten thousand persons. In the evening there was a reception at the Residency, which was attended by the Rajah and his chief Sirdars and officials, who seemed to enjoy much looking at the pictures, toys, &c., which were displayed for their amusement.

On the 26th October a great feast was given by the Rajah to the Sirdars and others, and with this entertainment the festivities consequent on the Rajah's adoption concluded.

SUPPLEMENT.

The Diary is obviously not a literary work, but a private memorandum-book, containing a brief record of names and dates and the chief events of each day. It has been printed as a memorial or relic of the young Prince, so prematurely cut off, for the sake of his friends and relations, who had eagerly looked forward to his return home and his account of his travels in Europe. It was at first intended that it should be privately printed, but on consideration there seemed to be no objection to publishing it, and thereby

SUPPLEMENT.

placing it within the reach of all who felt interested in the Rajah in this country or in India. On this point it may be well to quote the opinion of a high authority in Indian matters, Sir Bartle Frere, who observes in a private letter:—

"In this country the interest of the publication will rest mainly on the evidence it affords of a complete change, in one generation, from the Hindoo Rajahs who reigned at Kolhapoor within my own memory, making peace and war, rebelling and being conquered, in a very independent semi-civilized fashion, to the fairly educated Feudatory who gave so much promise of being at no distant date transformed into a very good Oriental copy of our European noblemen. From this point of view the book will be a very curious one, and will interest many. But in India the work will interest a much wider class of readers; and will probably be eagerly perused by all who read it in the Rajah's own class."

To show the impression the Rajah made in this country on cultivated people of the higher classes, regarding him from a purely English point of view, there is here appended (by permission) the greater part of Lady Verney's graphic article in *Good Words*, June, 1871:—

A YOUNG INDIAN PRINCE.

"In that strange 'fortuitous concourse of atoms' which streams perpetually from the most distant parts of the world into that Alexandria of the West—London the cosmopolitan—there came to us last summer a young Indian sovereign prince, the Maharajah of Kolhapoor.

"It was the first time that a reigning Hindoo had ever ventured to travel

SUPPLEMENT.

so far, and the journey was a great event among his people, who were much distressed at the idea of his crossing the sea. The whole undertaking was one, indeed, requiring a degree of resolution which it is difficult for us to realise. He belonged, however, to the Mahrattas, who are more enterprising than most races of Hindoos. He spoke English well, and had acquired a certain knowledge of modern history and of the politics and statesmen of the day, which enabled him to be interested in the conversation going on around him.

"He was barely twenty, though he looked much older; a small-made man, with extremely slender hands and feet; his complexion of that pleasantly brown colour which looks as if it had been just ripened by the sun, not scorched black; the eyes very large and lustrous, without much expression; and a contemplative, rather child-like look; his white teeth shone brilliantly, however, when he spoke, and lighted up the dark face.

"A kindly, gentle young prince, not wanting in intelligence, with a sort of easy dignity, as of one used to be obeyed, but apparently quite contented to remain languidly in the place where he happened to be, so that one wondered the more to see him venturing so far from home.

"He was ordinarily dressed in a kind of dark green cloth coat, with a curious edifice on his head formed of rolls of red muslin twisted into thin coils, without which he was never seen in public, any more than Louis XIV. without his wig. He would have considered it an act of rudeness on his part to show himself bareheaded, though he pulled off his turban when with his own people only. He had never been alone in all his life, and used to sit chatting and laughing with his attendants on terms of perfect ease, curiously mixed with the Oriental depth of respect and reverence with which they treated him.

"He was already married, and a child had been born to him just before his departure. 'Only a girl,' however, much to his disappointment, as a daughter could not inherit. The Mahrattas are monogamists; but sovereigns and very great chiefs are sometimes, though only for reasons of state policy, allowed by the 'sages' to take a second wife.

SUPPLEMENT.

"In the Rajah's case, a little extra princess, who is now about seven years old, was growing up in reserve for him. She was the daughter of a very ancient and noble family, the Naik Nimbalkur of Phultum (not far from Poona); a house which was said to have already reigned a thousand years at the time of the Mahometan invasion, and whose clan furnished many brave leaders to the Mahratta cause in the succeeding struggles.

"She is described by a lady who saw her some four years ago as a lovely little child about two years and a half old, who came in escorted with a great pomp of attendants. They bore a sort of canopy over her, nominally to protect her from the gaze of mankind as she descended from her gilt coach; but the decorum was only a sham, as she could be perfectly well seen under it. She was dressed in a short armless purple velvet jacket, and the *saree*, the long, graceful drapery worn by all Hindoos, wound about her. Her little arms and ankles were covered with bangles, she wore a large ring in her nose, and several pairs of earrings hung round the lobes of her ears. If she had been old enough for 'manners,' she would have inquired the ages of her visitors, and the ages of all their relations and friends, which is the correct style of conversation. As it was, her whole little soul was absorbed in a parasol, an instrument which she had never seen before, and which she kept opening and shutting with great delight all the time of her visit.

"'I shall bring the Ranee to see you in England,' Rajaram said to his English friends; but this was intended to refer to the mother of his child, not to this little lady.

"He had expressed a wish to see ordinary country life in England, and accordingly went to pay a visit in a country house. He came attended by three of his thirteen native servants, his English footman, and the English officer who accompanied him everywhere; but the accommodation required for the native suite was not excessive. The Rajah himself accepted a bed, but slept on the outside of it, wrapped in a magnificent pelisse of scarlet cloth embroidered with gold. The

SUPPLEMENT.

attendants lay in rugs on the floor, in their master's room and the dressing-room adjoining. His religious ablutions every morning were long and most scrupulously performed. Everything about him was kept with great cleanliness and nicety—but to be touched by no intrusive housemaid. There was at first some difficulty in the arrangements concerning food. Not only must the killing and the cooking be done by the hands of the orthodox, but the passing of the shadow of any but a 'twice born' * over the result, when prepared, would render it unfit to eat. All approach during these operations was warded off most energetically.

"A small garden house having been cleared out, Dunderbar, a tall, handsome fellow clad in brown cloth, with a red turban like his master's; the 'cook,' of a rather darker shade, in white garments with a red fez; and a third tall fellow, whom the English servants nicknamed 'the kitchen-maid,' in blue with a turban, encamped there with an immense chest which they brought with them. They built their charcoal fire in the corner, and established themselves beside it, squatting with their multitudinous copper vessels big and little, without handles, used alike to cook on the fire and to fetch water, as they would use none which they did not themselves draw at the well.

"They brought their own rice, spices, meat, and flour with them, and accepted nothing but live fowls, eggs, and vegetables; they were very liberal in giving away their food, to which the cloves, curry powder, &c., which they used for everything alike, gave a certain sameness of fiery taste almost intolerable to Western palates, but which was otherwise very good. They all ate with their fingers, but scrupulously washed their hands afterwards. The rest of the day the attendants sat munching cloves and nuts of various descriptions, smoking from a common pipe, which each passed on after taking a single whiff. One of them was always left on guard lest the vessels, &c., should be touched, and so defiled. They were extremely

---

* A twice born is a Brahmin, or a Chetrya, the two highest castes, or a man who has become so by penances or good works.

SUPPLEMENT.

intelligent, and showed themselves very quick in comprehending everything with little language but that of signs by those who had to deal with them.

"A morning room was given up to the Rajah, with an entrance on the garden, through which his meals were brought without danger of contamination—the cook in his white garments, his foot bare on the rough gravel, but his head scrupulously covered (Indian respect is shown in a way exactly the opposite of European manners), bearing in aloft on one hand, the arm bent back, a little tray covered with a napkin. The Rajah was extremely kind and courteous, making very pleasantly such pretty little speeches as his *métier* of prince required. He played eagerly at croquet, and the wide, green English lawn under the shadow of the trees was an oasis of common interest for the dusky little Eastern prince and the fair-haired, fair-complexioned Western girls and children, very curious to watch and consider amongst the dearth of points where intercourse was possible; while at a respectful distance his three attendants stood following the success of their master's strokes with extreme interest.

"It was strange to look on the 'mild Hindoo' and remember the fierce ancestry he came of. He was a collateral descendant of the great Mahratta chief Sivajee, the founder of the Mahratta Empire (in the days between our Restoration and Revolution), who bearded the power of the Mogul Emperors when at its highest, and rose upon its ruins. 'The little mountain rat,' as Aurungzebe contemptuously called him, won from the Great Mogul a territory on the western coast of India, extending one hundred and twenty miles in breadth and four hundred in length, from near Goa to near Bombay, and thence north, which Sivajee possessed at the time of his death, aged only fifty-two, in 1680.

"Kolhapour is in the Bombay presidency, situated on the western side of India, and consists mainly of a fertile plain lying east of the line of the Ghauts. Cotton, tobacco, and corn flourish in its deep black soil. Roads till within the last few years there were absolutely none. A nephew of the poet Southey, who crossed the territory some twenty-five years ago during the

SUPPLEMENT.

rains, wrote word that he had tried twenty-four different modes of crossing swollen rivers during his journey of one hundred and forty miles; among which were—1. Swimming with his clothes *on*; 2, with his clothes *off*, and upon his head; 3, on horseback; 4, on the ferryman's back; 5, on a basket; 6, on a door; 7, on a ladder; 8, on inflated skins; 9, on a netful of hollowed pumpkins; 10, holding a bullock's tail; 11, by a buffalo's tail, which is safer, inasmuch as he swims better than his fellow-beast, but requires a more wary hand upon him, since he is so fond of the water, that when he reaches the shore he is quite ready to turn round and swim back again. The last item in the list was a sugar-boiling pan; and there was but one bridge among the twenty-four ways, which was not, after all, in the territory of Kolhapoor, but in that of Sattara.

"Even quite lately, on a progress made four years ago by the last admirable Governor of Bombay, Sir Bartle Frere, to visit the Rajah who had adopted Rajaram, the edge of the cotton-fields was found a better line along which to drive and ride than the ordinary tracks. At night the party encamped in the open country, and when they reached the Kistna they crossed in circular wicker baskets made of cotton twigs covered with leather, which whirled round and round in the stream, while a body-guard of natives escorted them, swimming in all directions on inflated skins. Having once more resumed their march, the Governor and his daughter were met by the Rajah himself, with a magnificent procession of elephants and horses, in gala dress with splendid housings; the elephants with arabesques painted on their broad foreheads, and silver bangles on their post-like legs; the horses still more liberally adorned—one white horse had stripes of magenta painted over him, face and all.

"Everything was going on with great ceremony and decorum, when suddenly a baby elephant, which had accompanied its mother to increase the number and grandeur of the retinue, took fright—probably not having been used to so much company—and ran away. He was so small that he passed under the legs of the others, one of which had such an exceedingly bad temper

SUPPLEMENT.

that he was only brought out on great occasions, when every animal the state possessed was mustered. Offended at the liberty taken with his legs, he set off, regardless of hospitality, charging down on the English party. It was no joke. The heavy beast rushed on, swaying violently from side to side, as is the habit of elephants when they are angry, till he had thrown off his riders and twisted the howdah on one side. The mahout, however, held firm, seated on his head, and did not altogether lose control over him as he plunged into the crowd, nearly overturning Governor and suite, till at length the attendants succeeded in directing him into the harmless open country, and the whole procession once more resumed its decorum and its march to the town of Kolhapoor. It is a not very interesting collection of one-storied houses, chiefly of mud; the palace, a large square building, with a very handsome gateway, consisting of three deep horseshoe arches lined with beautiful fretwork, is built round a great courtyard, its walls adorned by gigantic frescoes in brilliant colouring of scenes from the Hindoo mythology, ' very startling and effective.'

" On the evening of the day of his arrival the Governor paid his return visit to the Maharajah. It was growing dusk, and the lines of streets were marked out by little lamps suspended from the ends of bamboos fastened to the tops of the houses—a most picturesque mode of aërial illumination; while flowers were scattered about in profusion. These are the great staple of Indian decoration, are cultivated for the purpose everywhere, and are always exquisitely arranged. Before the centre arch of the entrance to the palace stood two sentry-boxes, in each of which towered an elephant and his rider, a Brobdingnag edition of the sentinels at the Horse Guards, of a very grandiose description.

" The hall of ceremony where the Durbar was held was supported by columns covered with scarlet lac, like sealing-wax, the wall ornamented all round with the same, which looked extremely brilliant when lighted up. The Rajah sat at the head of a long line of followers up one side of the room, just opposite the Governor, who headed a similar line of his own suite, on the

SUPPLEMENT.

other side, and, as the hall was narrow, they were thus within speaking distance of each other without compromising the dignity of either. Both host and guest had garlands of flowers hung round them, necklaces of white jessamine, of the beautiful Stephanotus and sweet-smelling tuberoses strung on threads, five together, and fastened with a rose at intervals. Through a veiled door at the end the ladies of the zenana looked in and listened. An entertainment then followed in a hall lined with white marble throughout, with white marble columns and chairs of the same, set against the wall, and, of course, immovable. Sweetmeats mixed with flowers were laid out on a table, an innovation in honour of English customs. Within was another apartment belonging to the zenana, the decorations of which were all in black marble, with columns of black basalt, where the chief princess—in this case the Akasahib, a married sister of the Rajah's—did the honours to the Governor's daughter, 'assisted' more humbly by the Ranee. The wife is quite second in position in a Hindoo establishment while the mother and sister of the chief are alive, and to turn these out of a house would be looked upon as an act of cruelty not even to be thought of. Their family affection is often extremely strong, and the Akasahib, who followed her brother to the grave in a very short time, was supposed to have died of grief at his loss. The great man being expected patriarchally to shelter all his relations under his roof, the palace was honey-combed with a number of little courts for the different families, with small rooms entirely open on one side, and lighted only by this way, like those at Pompeii.

"The Rajah was exceedingly anxious that his adopted son, a young cousin, should inherit his dignity if he himself died without a lineal descendant, and the boy Rajaram was educated accordingly. He succeeded to the principality about two years ago. The little state contains about a million inhabitants, including feudatories, over whom the sovereign has power of life and death ; and a tolerably large revenue is collected from the inhabitants, thanks to its inexhaustibly fertile soil, where the same crops have come up on the same ground for centuries, without manure and without signs of failure.

SUPPLEMENT.

"About the beginning of last year the young prince determined to spend the time before reaching his majority in a pilgrimage to England, which he reached in June. He hired a house in London, and worked hard at seeing the sights required from a conscientious traveller: attended debates in both Houses of Parliament, was present at a Queen's ball in gorgeous apparel, where, in his cloth-of-gold tissues, necklaces, and strings of jewels, he looked like the prince in a fairy tale. He paid a visit to the Queen at Windsor, who, he said, 'was very kind;' attended a meeting of the British Association at Liverpool, where, being asked to speak, he said a few words, much to the satisfaction of his audience, on his intention to do all in his power to encourage the cultivation of cotton on his return to India; went into Scotland, where he distributed the prizes at a great volunteer festival, and made a second little speech, greatly to the purpose, about the good feeling growing up between East and West, and on the friendly relations of India to England. He ended by a visit to the Maharajah Duleep Singh, in Suffolk, which he is said to have much enjoyed. He seemed much pleased, altogether, with his treatment during his whole stay, and was turning his steps homeward to India through Belgium, the Tyrol, and Italy, the way by Paris, where he otherwise wished to have gone, being blocked by the war, when he was overtaken by the winter.

"The snow fell, and his followers were extremely anxious to carry back a box of the strange stuff to 'show them at home.' Even the moderate degree of cold in an English October had tried the men very painfully, and probably affected poor Rajaram himself. He was taken ill at Florence with a heart complaint, from which he had already suffered before at Innspruck on his journey. Nothing, probably, could have been of much use in such a case; he disliked being attended by Western physicians, and the end was very sudden at last, though the best doctors in Florence were summoned to his aid for the satisfaction of his most careful and judicious guardian, Captain West. Almost as soon as the breath was out of the Rajah's body, his poor attendants began their preparations, intending at first to burn it on the Lung'

SUPPLEMENT.

Arno, the very midst of the city, as the ceremony must be performed on the banks of a river. This, of course, could not be permitted, and with much difficulty Sir Augustus Paget obtained permission from the Italian authorities to allow the funeral to be carried out after midnight, at the end of the Cascine, two miles from the town.

"It was a dark night; a blustering north wind was blowing, and the cold was biting, says an eye-witness; the pile had been built already breast-high, and near it was a fire, round which a group of Hindoos were standing sadly and silently. 'The Rajah was the kindest and best of masters, and these poor fellows are as grieved at his loss as if he were their own father,' was the affectionate tribute of his English servant.

"Presently came up an omnibus containing the body, which was then brought out upon a plank. As it was borne along, the light from two feeble lanterns fell on the placid features of a young and apparently corpulent man. The turban and a richly-embroidered robe which wrapped the corpse were of bright scarlet; the bracelets, necklaces, and jewels round his neck and arms were said to be of great value, and were all afterwards consumed in the fire. The body was then laid reverentially upon the pile. One attendant placed betel-nut in the mouth and hands, a second piled camphor around it, another muttered several prayers. A Brahmin priest performed strange ceremonies with a white linen cloth, which he folded and unfolded, offering up prayers while kneading dough, to be placed alongside the corpse, which was then carefully fenced in with logs and planks, forming a sort of box, into which were thrown perfumes and essences; fresh logs were piled up for about a couple of yards more; camphor, and a mixture of beeswax and turpentine, and a quantity of brushwood and shavings, were added, and the mass was then kindled. The flames shot up brilliantly, driven by a strong gust of wind, throwing a lurid glare on the numerous spectators, the muddy Arno, the black clumps of trees, not yet quite bare of leaves, and the groups of Indians of every different shade of colour from coal black to light brown, with their glistening white teeth, and turbans differing in shape according to the rank of the

SUPPLEMENT.

wearers. Each had his settled station near the funeral fire, and stood gazing intently on it during the long cold hours with a kind of mournful forlorn resignation which was extremely touching—many of them weeping bitterly. At seven in the morning the wood was all consumed, the embers were extinguished by water from the river, the ashes were collected and placed in a porcelain jar to be carried home. Everything used in the funeral pile was then taken out in a boat and sunk in mid-stream, and the attendants laid fresh earth on the spot itself, traced in the form of a heart, around which were then placed small vessels containing rice. Then all the Hindoos knelt and prayed with their faces to the ground—the dismal ceremony was finished, and the forlorn retinue departed in silence, bearing with them the vase with the ashes to be thrown into the Ganges, when they should reach their native land. The next day they had all left Florence.

"And thus, far from his Indian, and even his English friends, his country, his young wife and child, amongst men of an alien religion, of foreign and unsympathising race, the poor boy Rajah passed away. His death is a real misfortune, and very seriously to be regretted for every reason. It is sad to think of the dismay and grief it will occasion in his family and his state; and it is to be feared that it will discourage men of his class, who might otherwise undertake the journey to Europe, from attempting so dangerous an experiment. Rajaram had made a great effort to visit England, and seemed quite disposed to use his experience on his return to Kolhapoor, and introduce many reforms, especially with regard to the education of women. He 'wished particularly,' he said, 'to have the Ranee instructed.' And this is a change which may be said to lie at the root of all real improvement in India. While the zenana remains what it is, the lowering effect of its atmosphere upon the men of the higher classes, in childhood and manhood alike, is almost as injurious as to the women themselves.

"'I was born in this courtyard, I have lived and been married in this court, and in this court I shall die,' said a poor Hindoo princess, who longed after better things, with a sort of groan."

SUPPLEMENT.

The writer concludes by noticing—

"How affectionately Rajaram spoke of the kindness shown to him in England, how much he seemed to enjoy his visit, and how true an interest was shown in his welfare, and what sorrow for his fate has been felt by all classes who came in contact, during his stay, with the gentle, kindly young Maharajah of Kolhapoor."

A few slight and inevitable inaccuracies occur here and there in the above article, which it has not been thought necessary to correct. In some cases (*e.g.* as to the funeral details) the preceding pages supply the corrections required.

It only remains to add, that the design on the covers of the book is copied from a letter of the Rajah's. The following explanation of it is furnished by the kindness of Sir Bartle Frere:—

"The device on the Rajah's note-paper is a belt, including a pair of 'Mohrchails,' or peacock-feather fans, or fly-flappers, which, according to old custom in India, and, I believe, elsewhere in the East, are the emblems either of independent sovereignty or of one invested by an emperor with royal powers. They are gold-mounted, and are borne on each side of the possessor on all state occasions. The pair used by the Rajah of Kolhapoor were granted by the Emperor of Delhi, and were highly valued, as very few princes could boast such a grant. I believe the peacock-feather fans borne on state occasions before the Pope are of Oriental origin, but the feathers are differently set."

The home Editor, who undertook to see the book through the press, is responsible for the foregoing Supplement.

January 3, 1872.

LONDON:
PRINTED BY SMITH, ELDER AND CO.,
OLD BAILEY, E. C.

www.ingramcontent.com/pod-product-compliance
Lightning Source LLC
Chambersburg PA
CBHW020253170426
43202CB00008B/348